Introduction

Two JASDF F-4EJ(KAI) Phantoms taxi back to their dispersal. (Emil Cooper)

Rhino, Toom, Smoker, Old Smokey, Lead Sled and Double-Ugly are all F-4 nicknames; few military aircraft have drawn such polarized feelings, attitudes and opinions as the McDonnell Douglas F-4 Phantom II. Whoever you ask: aircrew, ground crew, scale modellers and enthusiasts, almost all have an opinion to offer, much like Marmite sandwich spread, you either love it, or you hate it.

Personally, I love the F-4, always have, and in recent years it has taken over my number one slot for favourite aircraft of all time from the English Electric Lightning. The sheer brute power and acceleration are frankly awesome. As a small boy my parents took me to RAF Biggin Hill air displays in the UK and I experienced up close the raw power, noise and thunder as the F-4 pilot plugged in the burners and hauled that immense Phantom airframe around the tight circuit that is 'Biggin on the Bump', a nod to its location. How could anyone fail to be moved by such a spectacle?

Robert Prest was an RAF FGR-2 Phantom pilot stationed in Germany at the height of the Cold War. His book, *F-4 Phantom: A Pilot's Story*, is a riveting read that gives a real sense of the drama, tension and belief that it wasn't a matter of *if* the Russians were coming, but *when.*

This book charts the birth, adolescence and adulthood of one of the most important military aircraft to see active service. Inevitably, any book is limited in terms of extent and so I have done my best to include as great a variety as possible in terms of different F-4 variants and scale models. It has been impossible to include everything. What follows is inevitably summative and inevitably seeks to capture the essential details relating to the F-4 Phantom.

Port view of two F-4S Phantom IIs from Fighter Squadron (VF)-301, 'Devil's Disciples', NAS Miramar.

So much has been written about the F-4 Phantom II that's it's an honour to bring together an historical summary of this famous supersonic and a range of unique scale modelling projects to whet the appetite.

It's hard to imagine any other combat jet that's more recognizable than the McDonnell Douglas F-4 Phantom II; a tandem two-seat, twin-engine, all-weather, long-range supersonic jet interceptor and fighter-bomber originally developed for the United States Navy by McDonnell Aircraft. It first entered service in 1961 with the US Navy. Proving highly adaptable, it was also adopted by the United States Marine Corps and the United States Air Force, and by the mid-1960s had become a major part of their air arms and went on to sell widely across the world. Phantom production ran from 1958 to 1981, with a total of 5,195 units built, making it the most-produced American supersonic military aircraft. Multiple upgrades have been incorporated into the type to keep it at the forefront of its capability, such as the F-4E 2020 Terminator operated by the Turkish Air Force.

The Phantom is a large fighter with a top speed of over Mach 2.2. It can carry more than 18,000 pounds (8,400kg) of weapons on nine external hard points, including air-to-air missiles, air-to-ground missiles, and various bombs. The F-4, like other interceptors of its time, was initially designed without an internal cannon. Later models incorporated an M61 Vulcan rotary cannon. Beginning in 1959, it set 15 world records for inflight performance, including an absolute speed record and an absolute altitude record.

On 27 May 1958, the F-4H-1 development aircraft took to the skies over St Louis, piloted by Robert C. Little, flying solo. Few would have believed the success that would unfold for the type over the coming 60-plus years of service.

We know today that the F-4 Phantom II became the standard against which every other fighter of its generation would be measured. The F-4 has seen much combat in its lifetime and was used extensively during the Vietnam War. It served as the principal air superiority fighter for the US Air Force, Navy, and Marine Corps, and became important in the ground-attack and aerial-reconnaissance roles late in that war. During the Vietnam years, one US Air Force pilot, two weapon systems officers (WSOs), one US Navy pilot and one radar intercept officer (RIO) became aces by achieving five aerial kills against enemy fighter aircraft. The F-4 continued to form a major part of US military air power throughout the 1970s and 1980s, being gradually replaced by more modern aircraft such as the F-15 Eagle and F-16 Fighting Falcon in the US Air Force, the F-14 Tomcat in the US Navy and the F/A-18 Hornet in the US Navy and US Marine Corps.

The F-4 Phantom II remained in use by the US in the reconnaissance and Wild Weasel (Suppression of Enemy Air Defences) roles in the 1991 Gulf War, finally leaving service in 1996. It was also the only aircraft used by both US flight demonstration teams: the United States Air Force Thunderbirds (F-4E) and the United States Navy Blue Angels (F-4J). The F-4 was also operated by the armed forces of 11 other nations. Israeli Phantoms saw extensive combat in several Arab–Israeli conflicts, while Iran used its large fleet of Phantoms, acquired before the fall of the Shah, in the Iran–Iraq War of the 1980s.

Speed is crucial to any fighter aircraft and the Phantom's greatest advantage in air combat was acceleration and thrust, which permitted a skilled pilot to engage and disengage from the fight at will. MiGs could usually outturn the F-4 because of the high drag on its airframe; as a massive fighter aircraft designed to fire radar-guided missiles from beyond visual range, the F-4 lacked the agility of its Soviet opponents and was subject to adverse yaw during hard manoeuvring. Although thus subject to irrecoverable spins during aileron rolls, pilots reported the aircraft to be very responsive and easy to fly on the edge of its performance envelope. In 1972 the F-4E model was upgraded with leading-edge slats on the wings, greatly improving high angle-of-attack manoeuvrability at the expense of top speed.

The lack of an internal gun 'was the biggest mistake on the F-4', according to John Cheshire, a US Navy pilot: 'Bullets are cheap and tend to go where you aim them. I needed a gun, and I really wished I had one.' Marine Corps General John R. Dailey recalled that 'everyone in RF-4s wished they had a gun on the aircraft'.

The first US Navy McDonnell YF-4H-1 Phantom II (BuNo 142259) taking off in September 1959. This aircraft made its first flight on 27 May 1958 but crashed on 21 October 1959 at Edwards Air Force Base, California, USA, while attempting a new height record (Project Top Flight), killing the McDonnell test pilot 'Zeke' Hoelsbeck.

The lack of a cannon was finally addressed by adding an internally mounted 20mm (0.79in) M61A1 Vulcan on the F-4E.

On 6 December 1959, while flying another YF-4H-1, Commander Lawrence E. Flint established an absolute manned-flight altitude record of 96,566ft (30,040m) as part of Project Top Flight. This marque eclipsed by nearly 4,000 feet (1,220m) the record previously held by a Soviet aircraft.

The designers Barkey and Timms worked closely as the design went through the usual ups and downs; on 26 May 1955, they settled on a two-man crew for the new aircraft and its designation was changed from AH-1 to F-4H-1. In July a detailed list of specifications was adopted for the aircraft and the McDonnell design was now slated to have twin J79 engines, AAM-N-6 Sparrow III radar-missile armament, improved air-intercept radar, a maximum speed of at least Mach 2 and a the two-man crew. The navy committed to the purchase of two prototypes (BuNos 142259 and 142260) and at the same time authorized Vought to build two prototypes of the single-seat, single-engine, missile-carrying F8U-3 Crusader III to compete with the McDonnell design.

The flight surfaces of the new aircraft did not evolve, contrary to legend, from someone trampling on the blueprints. The original AH-1 had a low-set tailplane, but in the F-4H-1 there was no place to situate it. After much wind tunnel work and consideration of more than 20 designs, it was decided to apply 23 degrees of anhedral. This gave the necessary degree of stability but still left the tailplane free of the jet efflux. This configuration contributed in the development phase to stall-recovery problems.

The wing underwent many changes. The centre section of the wing had been envisioned as an immensely strong unit, spanning 27ft (8.23m) from wing fold to wing fold with a permanent manufacturing splice at the centreline. Barkey's engineers reached a point where, to avoid having to redesign the entire wing, they gave the outboard panels 12 degrees of dihedral, resulting in an 'average' wing dihedral of 5 degrees. In this remarkably casual manner, the wing shape of the future Phantom was determined. The maiden flight was postponed several times, eventually being accomplished on 27 May 1958, with Bob Little at the controls.

Incredibly, at the time of writing, 63 years after its first flight, the F-4 has only just been retired from active service with the Japan Air Self-Defense Force (JASDF) and is still operational elsewhere; Turkey operates F-4E models upgraded to 'Terminator 2020' standard, Greece and South Korea also operate F-4E models and Iran operates a few F-4D, F-4E and RF-4E models.

Phantom II production ended in the United States in 1979 after 5,195 had been built (5,057 by McDonnell Douglas and 138 in Japan by Mitsubishi). A span of 23 years' continuous production. Of these 2,874 went to the USAF, 1,264 to the Navy and Marine Corps, and the rest to foreign customers. The last US-built F-4s went to South Korea, while the last F-4 ever built was an F-4EJ built by Mitsubishi Heavy Industries in Japan and was delivered on 20 May 1981. As of 2008, 631 Phantoms were in service worldwide; Phantoms were in use as a target drone (specifically QF-4Cs) operated by the US military until 21 December 2016 when the Air Force officially ended use of the type.

From 1961 when the Phantom II became operational with the USN until superseded by the Grumman F-14 Tomcat in the 1980s, the type had served on every US super-carrier of the period, both in the Pacific and Atlantic theatres of operations.

The aircraft's emblem is a whimsical cartoon ghost called 'The Spook', which was created by McDonnell Douglas technical artist, Anthony Wong, for shoulder patches. The name 'Spook' was coined by the crews

A US Navy McDonnell F-4H-1 Phantom II of Fighter Squadron VF-74 'Be-Devilers' assigned to Carrier Air Group 8 (CVG-8) aboard the aircraft carrier *USS Forrestal* (CVA-59) pictured taking off from an unidentified airfield. On 8 July 1961 VF-74 began transitioning into the airplane, thus becoming the first deployable Phantom squadron in the US Navy.

This 1,000 hours in a F-4 Phantom patch illustrates the Spook

of either the 12th Tactical Fighter Wing or the 4453rd Combat Crew Training Wing at MacDill Air Force Base (AFB). The figure is ubiquitous, appearing on many items associated with the F-4.

The US Navy led a series of record-breaking flights early in Phantom development; in all, the Phantom set 16 world records. Except for Operation Skyburner, all records were achieved in unmodified production aircraft. Five of the speed records remained unbeaten until the F-15 Eagle appeared in 1975. During Operation Skyburner on 22 November 1961, a modified Phantom with water injection, piloted by Lieutenant-Colonel Robert B. Robinson, set an absolute world record average speed over a 20-mile (32.2km) -long two-way straight course of 1,606.342 mph (2,585.086 km/h).

To mark the 60th anniversary of the original transatlantic crossing on 1 June 1979 two Royal Air Force McDonnell Douglas Phantom FGR.2s – XV424 (of 56 Squadron) and RAF Coningsby-based XV486, were sprayed in special commemorative schemes. The scheme was designed by aviation artist Wilfred Hardy, commonly known for his impressive cover artwork on Royal Air Force yearbooks. As well as marking the anniversary of the crossing, the scheme also made reference to usage of Rolls-Royce engines in both aircraft: the Rolls-Royce Eagle in the Vimy and the Rolls-Royce Spey in the Phantom FGR.2. In addition to this it also marked the 30th anniversary of the North Atlantic Treaty Organization (NATO).

The Phantom FGR.2 (XV424), which made the crossing, departing from the International Air Tattoo in 1979. (Mike Freer, *Touchdown Aviation*)

It was decided that XV424 would make the flight and that XV486 would serve as backup. On 19 June, XV424 departed from RAF St. Athan to CFB Goose Bay from where the crossing would be made. The crew chosen for the crossing were: Squadron Leader A.J.N. Alcock (pilot and nephew of Sir John Alcock who made the original crossing) and Flight Lieutenant W.N. Browne (navigator). For the journey the pair brought with them Brown's original toy cat mascot 'Twinkle Toes'.

On 21 June, XV424 took off from Goose Bay, Labrador, and began the crossing to Ireland. Flying subsonically the entire time, the journey took 5 hours and 40 minutes, setting a new record. The Phantom was refuelled five times throughout the crossing by Handley Page Victor K.2 tankers of 57 Squadron. Today XV424 is preserved at the RAF Hendon, sporting colours of 56 (Fighter) Squadron, while XV486 was scrapped in 1993.

The USAF and the US Navy had high expectations of the F-4 Phantom, assuming that the massive firepower, the best available on-board radar, the highest speed and acceleration properties, coupled with new tactics, would provide Phantoms with an advantage over the MiGs. However, in confrontations with the lighter MiG-21, F-4s did not always succeed and began to suffer losses. Over the course of the air war in Vietnam, between 3 April 1965 and 8 January 1973, each side would ultimately claim favourable kill ratios.

During the war, US Navy F-4 Phantoms claimed 40 air-to-air victories at a loss of 7 Phantoms to enemy aircraft. USMC F-4 pilots claimed 3 enemy MiGs at a cost of one aircraft in air combat. USAF F-4 Phantom crews scored 107.5 MiG kills (including 33.5 MiG-17s, eight MiG-19s and 66 MiG-21s) at a cost of 33 Phantoms in air combat. F-4 pilots were credited with a total of 150.5 MiG kills at a cost of 42 Phantoms in air combat.

According to the Vietnam People's Air Force (VPAF), 103 F-4 Phantoms were shot down by MiG-21s at a cost of 54 MiG-21s downed by F-4s. During the war, the VPAF lost 131 MiGs in air combat (63 MiG-17s, eight MiG-19s and 60 MiG-21s) of which half were by F-4s.

From 1966 to November 1968, in 46 air battles conducted over North Vietnam between F-4s and MiG-21s, the VPAF claimed 27 F-4s were shot down by MiG-21s at a cost of 20 MiG-21s. In 1970, one F-4 Phantom was shot down by a MiG-21. The struggle culminated on 10 May 1972

Hellenic Air Force RF-4E Phantom II (serial 7487), in a special colour scheme, lands at the Royal International Air Tattoo, Fairford, Gloucestershire, England. (Adrian Pingstone)

with VPAF aircraft completing 64 sorties, resulting in 15 air battles. The VPAF claimed 7 F-4s were shot down, while the US confirmed only 5 F-4s were lost. The Phantoms, in turn, managed to destroy 2 MiG-21s, 3 MiG-17s and 1 MiG-19. On 11 May, two MiG-21s, which played the role of bait, guided four F-4s onto 2 MiG-21s circling at low altitude. The MiGs quickly engaged and shot down 2 F-4s. On 18 May, Vietnamese aircraft made 26 sorties in 8 air engagements, which cost 4 F-4 Phantoms; Vietnamese fighters on that day did not suffer losses.

A US Navy McDonnell Douglas F-4J Phantom II from Fighter Squadron VF-74 'Be-Devilers' is prepared for launch during flight operations aboard the attack aircraft carrier USS *America* (CVA-66). VF-74 was assigned to Attack Carrier Air Wing 8 (CVW-8) aboard the *America* for a deployment to Vietnam from 5 June 1972 to 24 March 1973. In the background is a Sikorsky SH-3G Sea King helicopter from helicopter combat support squadron HC-2 Det. 66 'Fleet Angels'.

Design & Development

A US Navy McDonnell F-4H-1 Phantom II (BuNo 148381, later re-designated F-4B-6-MC) from Fighter Squadron VF-74 'Be-Devilers' in flight, 1961. VF-74 was the first operational F-4 Phantom squadron and was assigned to Carrier Air Group 8 (CVG-8) aboard the aircraft carrier USS *Forrestal* (CVA-59).

Two US Navy McDonnell F-4B-19-MC Phantom II (BuNo 151474, 151491) of Fighter Squadron VF-84 'Jolly Rogers' in flight. VF-84 was assigned to Carrier Air Wing 7 (CVW-7) aboard the aircraft carrier USS *Independence* (CVA-62), 1 November 1964.

Two US Marine Corps McDonnell F-4B Phantom IIs (BuNos 150476, 152252) of Marine Fighter Attack Squadron VMFA-531 'Gray Ghosts' aboard the aircraft carrier USS *Forrestal* (CVA-59), in February 1973. VMFA-531 was assigned to Carrier Air Wing 17 (CVW-17) aboard the *Forrestal* for a deployment to the Mediterranean Sea from 22 September 1972 to 6 July 1973. From 23 February to 6 March 1973, VMFA-531's F-4B 151477, tail code AA-207, operated from the Royal Navy carrier HMS *Ark Royal* (R09). During that time it carried the squadron markings of No. 892 Squadron, *Ark Royal*'s F-4K squadron, on its fin.

US Navy: From prototype to F-4B

Commander Julian S. Lake had the historic task of leading his squadron, VF-74 'Be-Devilers', in becoming the first fleet squadron to operate the F-4H-1 Phantom. His task was to manage a fly-off with the Convair F-106 Delta Dart that included head-to-heads at extraordinary closing speeds – Mach 4 on occasion.

The new fighter-bomber embarked on one of the navy's newest carriers, USS *Forrestal* (CVA-59)

There were 47 pre-production jets that were given the designation F-4H-1F, while those that followed received the designation F-4H-1. This may have appeared confusing, given that the pre-production aircraft had little in common. Notably, from the 19th aircraft onwards, aircraft featured the raised canopy and were fitted with an AN/APQ-72 32in (81cm) radar and are just the same as production aircraft. An important development occurred on 1 October 1962 when the F-4H-1 was designated F-4B.

The US Navy wasn't the only service interested in the F-4B; the US Marine Corps, although not as large as the navy, was an elite force that wanted to take advantage of the firepower Phantom aircraft offered. VMFA-115 'Silver Eagles' used this version and with the aircraft was able to carry a large load of bombs and was ideal for air-to-ground missions. Competition was centre stage with both VMF(AW)-531 'Gray Ghosts' and VMF(AW)-314 'Black Knights' claiming to be the first F-4 squadron.

With American involvement in Vietnam increasing, F-4Bs of the VMFA-531 'Gray Ghosts' were the first Marine aircraft to deploy to Da Nang in April 1965.

Three-hundred-and-twenty F-4 Phantoms were in service with the US Navy by summer 1964 when the first of their type saw action in Vietnam as Vietnamese People's Navy (VPN) patrol boats were spotted. It was thought that they posed a great threat to USS *Maddox* and luckily the US Navy had four Phantom squadrons close by to call on: VF-96 'Fighting Falcons' and VF-92 'Silver Kings' on board USS *Ranger* (CVW-9) with VF-142 'Ghost Riders' and VF-143 'Pukin' Dogs' aboard USS *Constellation*.

A US Navy McDonnell F-4B-21-MC Phantom II (BuNo 152218) of Fighter Squadron VF-21 'Free Lancers' flying in Vietnam. VF-21 was assigned to Carrier Air Wing 2 (CVW-2) aboard the aircraft carrier USS *Midway* (CVA-41) for a deployment to Vietnam from 6 March to 23 November 1965. The aircraft is armed with two AIM-9B Sidewinder missiles and an AIM-7 Sparrow.

Marine Corps F-4Bs carried 500lb bombs, Zuni rockets and napalm. VMFA-323 was the first F-4 unit to lose an aircraft when F-4B BuNo 152261 took a hit from a surface-to-air missile (SAM). Crewed by Squadron XO Major John H. Dunn and his RIO, John Frederick, their F-4B went down on a night reconnaissance mission over North Vietnam. Both survived their ejection and were taken prisoner by North Vietnamese forces and although Major Dunn survived seven years in captivity, John Frederick died five years after their capture.

By 1975 the last of the F-4Bs were retired from USN service and placed in storage. The majority of the F-4Bs were replaced by later examples of the type such as the F-4J, F-4N and F-4S.

One significant feature of the early F-4s, notably the F-4B, was their bright colour schemes – they were certainly 'high-vis'. The reasons for this are many, notably the fierce loyalty and emotional attachment that all personnel have for their squadron and in part the very different schemes and symbols emblazoned on their F-4s reflect this. Just take a look at the impressive scale model of the Tamiya F-4B by George Canare in the modelling section of this book and the box scheme featuring a bird from VF-51 'Screaming Eagles' – simply incredible. Some of the most colourful airframes were (and still are) reserved for CAG (Commander Air Group) personal mounts. Initially and during the Second World War, the commander of the air group was the most senior officer of the embarked squadrons and was expected to personally lead all major strike operations, coordinating the

Above: A US Navy McDonnell F-4B-23-MC Phantom II (BuNo 152295) of Fighter Squadron 41 (VF-41) 'Black Aces' in flight. VF-41 was assigned to Carrier Air Wing 6 (CVW-6) aboard the aircraft carrier USS *Franklin D. Roosevelt* (CVA-42). 152295 was later converted to an F-4N and retired to the Military Aircraft Storage and Disposition Centre (MASDC) as FP0482 on 19 October 1983.

Left: Two US Navy McDonnell F-4B Phantom IIs of Fighter Squadron VF-111 'Sundowners' in flight, circa 1972. VF-111 was assigned to Carrier Air Wing 15 (CVW-15) aboard the aircraft carrier USS *Coral Sea* (CVA-43).

Four US Navy McDonnell F-4B Phantom IIs (BuNos 149460, 150450, 151430, 152208) of Fighter Squadron VF-14 'Tophatters' in flight. Operating the F-4B, VF-14 was assigned to Carrier Air Wing 1 (CVW-1) aboard the aircraft carrier USS *John F. Kennedy* (CVA-67) from November 1968 to December 1973. This photo was taken before 1973, as 149460 was retired to the MASDC as 8F0027 on 17 December 1972; 150450 was written off on 26 November 1973 while in service with VMFA-323; 151430 was converted to an F-4N and was still in use as a ground target at China Lake in 2007. 152208 was converted to an F-4N and retired to the MASDC as 8F0101 on 12 March 1982.

attacks of the carrier's fighter, bomber and torpedo planes in combat. The CAG was a department head of the ship reporting to the carrier's commanding officer. In 1963 when Carrier Air Groups were retitled Wings, the commander retained the legacy title of CAG, a tradition that continues to this day. Other reasons for such brightly painted military aircraft have included early, easier identification by friendly forces. Perhaps more controversially, aircraft painted in such bright schemes could make a political statement with an ability to project air power during the Cold War that said to any potential foe: look what we have, a jet more powerful and capable than anything that you may choose to send against us, what need have we for camouflage?

A US Navy McDonnell F-4J Phantom II from Fighter Squadron VF-33 'Tarsiers' in flight, 1979. VF-33 was assigned to Carrier Air Wing 6 (CVW-6) aboard the aircraft carrier USS *Independence* (CV-62) for a deployment to the Mediterranean from 28 June to 14 December 1979. Note the carrier names painted on the tail of F-4J-33-MC 155552: Kennedy, America, Nimitz, Eisenhower and Independence.

US Navy: F-4J

4 June 1965 was significant in F-4 development terms with the first flight of a converted F-4B (BuNo 151473) designated YF-4J, marking eight years since that first flight of the Phantom prototype with Bob Little in the front seat. The F-4J featured the drooped ailerons and slotted stabilizers of late production F-4B aircraft. These modifications helped reduce approach speeds on carrier deck landings to 125kts. Perhaps the greatest improvement that came with the F-4J model was the introduction of the AN/AWG-10 missile control system. The unit had a pulse-Doppler look-down capability as well as pulse search and track.

By February 1967 the F-4J was rapidly replacing the F-4B in squadron service. Although VF-84 'Jolly Rogers' was the first WestPac squadron to receive the F-4J, VF-33 'Tarsiers' scored the first MiG kill on 10 July 1968.

The Vietnam War dragged on and by the end of the conflict the Marines and US Navy had 448 Phantoms on strength that included no less than 21 squadrons operating the F-4J.

A US Navy McDonnell F-4J-47-MC Phantom II (BuNo 158378) from Fighter Squadron VF-21 'Free Lancers' in flight over Southern California, USA, 1974. VF-21 was assigned to Carrier Air Wing 2 (CVW-2) aboard the aircraft carrier USS *Ranger* (CVA-61) for a deployment to the Western Pacific from 7 May to 18 October 1974. This aircraft was also the personal aircraft of the commander of CVW-2.

A US Navy McDonnell F-4J-33-MC Phantom II (BuNo 155536) from Fighter Squadron VF-33 'Tarsiers', 1972. VF-33 was assigned to Carrier Air Wing 7 (CVW-7) aboard the aircraft carrier USS *Independence* (CVA-62).

A US Navy McDonnell F-4J Phantom II of Fighter Squadron VF-21 'Free Lancers' and a F-4J of VF-154 'Black Knights' in flight, circa 1970. Both squadrons were assigned to Carrier Air Wing 2 (CVW-2) aboard the aircraft carrier USS *Ranger* (CVA-61).

Four US Marine Corps McDonnell F-4J Phantom II (BuNo 153848, 155523, 155525, 155511) from Marine Fighter Attack Squadron VMFA-333 'Shamrocks' in flight. VMFA-333 was assigned to Carrier Air Wing 8 (CVW-8) aboard the aircraft carrier USS *Nimitz* (CVN-68) for a deployment to the Mediterranean Sea from 7 July 1976 to 7 February 1977.

A US Navy McDonnell F-4J-32-MC Phantom II (BuNo 153879) of Fighter Squadron VF-194 'Red Lightnings'. Note the experimental camouflage. Different camouflage schemes were tested, including one by Keith Ferris with his 'angular' camouflage pattern applied to an F-4C (63-7411). A similar scheme is applied to a US Navy F-4J (BuNo 153879).

A US Navy McDonnell Douglas F-4J Phantom II (BuNo 155895) of Fighter Squadron 96 (VF-96) 'Fighting Falcons' in flight over the aircraft carrier USS *Constellation* (CVA-64). VF-96 was assigned to Attack Carrier Air Wing 9 (CVW-9) aboard the *Constellation* between 1971 and 1974. The aircraft is fully armed with AIM-7 Sparrow and AIM-9D Sidewinder missiles, indicating that this photo was probably taken during deployment to Vietnam.

A McDonnell Douglas F-4J Phantom II (BuNo 157248) of fighter squadron VF-114 'Aardvarks' on the aircraft carrier USS *Kitty Hawk (CVA-63)* during a deployment to Vietnam between 6 November 1970 and 17 July 1971. The aircraft is armed with AIM-9D Sidewinder and AIM-7 Sparrow air-to-air missiles. Note the extended inflight refuelling probe. The aircraft was later converted to the F-4S standard and retired to the MASDC as 8F0201 on 16 August 1985.

As you might expect, development continued apace with advances that allowed the pilot to track and control Sparrow air-to-air missiles (AAMs) by line of sight. Pilots were able to do this using a Honeywell Visual Target Acquisition System (VTAS) that consisted of a helmet-mounted sight for missile lock-on. Arguably one of the most pilot-friendly advances in the F-4J came with the introduction of an Automatic Carrier Landing System (ACLS) making for much less stress for the crew when landing on deck, especially during the hours of darkness.

Development of a replacement for the F-4 was well underway by the early 1970s, although its replacement, the Grumman F-14 Tomcat. was a complex aircraft and inevitable delays ensued. To counter this, the F-4N and F-4S were developments of the F-4B and F-4J respectively.

US Navy: F-4N

F-4B BuNo 153034 was used as the F-4N development aircraft, taking to the air from the Naval Air Rework Facility North Island (NARF Noris) on 14 June 1972. There had been some concern by 1970 regarding the condition of its fleet of F-4Bs, many of which were over ten years old and showing signs of age and fatigue. Carrier operations take a heavy toll on aircraft deployed at sea and touch-up paint and a heavily worn look was common on aircraft ranged across the flight decks of US carriers at that time, and still is today. In that year, a programme named Bee Line was initiated in which F-4Bs were refurbished and modernized. This facility upgraded 227 airframes in total under the Bee Line programme and, interestingly, a few F-4Ns designated F-4N(AC) featured leading-edge slats with airframes supplied to the Marines.

Aircraft selected for conversion were sent to NAS (Naval Air Station) North Island, California, where they were stripped and inspected. They were then completely rebuilt using new parts. The changes included a structural strengthening to extend the fatigue life, plus a complete rewiring. The electrical generating system was upgraded with 30kVa constant speed alternators. The F-4N retained the thin wings and tyres; the main radar and the infrared search and track detector fitted under the nose radome of the F-4B. All F-4Ns had their inboard leading-edge flaps locked shut – a feature to note if you are building a scale model of the type.

The F-4N was fitted with Sanders AN/ALQ-126 or -126B deceptive electronic countermeasures equipment. This included long antenna fairings mounted on the sides of the upper air intakes. These fairings were the distinctive features which enabled F-4Ns to be externally distinguished from F-4Bs. The DECM antennae were in longer fairings than those used by the same equipment on the F-4J because of the difficulty in routing the cables. Radar homing and warning antennae for the ALQ-126 DECM were fitted to the undersides of the intakes and wings – just aft of the undercarriage bays. These were tied into the antennae on the trailing edge – and sometimes on the leading edge as well – of the vertical fin. There were other changes that included

A US Navy McDonnell F-4N Phantom II fighter (BuNo 151008) from Fighter Squadron VF-111 'Sundowners' being catapulted from the aircraft carrier USS *Franklin D. Roosevelt* (CV-42) in February 1977. VF-111 was assigned to Carrier Air Wing 19 (CVW-19) for FDR's final cruise to the Mediterranean Sea from 4 October 1976 to 21 April 1977. USS *Franklin D. Roosevelt* was decommissioned on 30 September 1977.

A US Navy Reserve McDonnell F-4N Phantom II (BuNo 151475) of Fighter Squadron VF-302 in flight over Marine Corps Air Station Yuma, Arizona, USA, in 1979.

A US Navy Reserve McDonnell F-4N Phantom II from Fighter Squadron 301 (VF-301) in flight over Naval Air Station San Diego, California, USA, 1980, where a Naval Air Rework Facility was located.

a helmet sight Visual Target Acquisition System (VTAS) and a Sidewinder Expanded Acquisition Mode (SEAM). A new dogfight mission computer was provided, together with auto-altitude reporting equipment. APX-76 or APX-80 air-to-air IFF equipment was fitted, plus AN/ASW-25 one-way datalink. The J79-GE-8 engines of the F-4B were retained, although smoke abatement equipment was fitted.

US Navy: F-4S

The F-4S was something of a 'hot rod' and its speed proved too risky to land on the smaller Midway-class aircraft carriers, meaning that VF-21 Freelancers and VF-154 Black Knights reverted to the F-4N for their final Phantom deployments. The F-4S had manoeuvring slats that took 12kts off the landing speed; their real improvement came by improving turn

A view of the tail section of a Marine Fighter Attack Squadron 321 (VMFA-321) F-4S Phantom II aircraft on display at the 1991 Department of Defense Joint Services Open House. VMFA-321 is a reserve squadron with the 4th Marine Aircraft Wing (4th MAW), Andrews Air Force Base.

The Golden Crown and Blue Angels aerobatic teams in Tehran, Iran, in June 1973. Six Northrop F-5E Tiger IIs of the Golden Crown team and six McDonnell Douglas F-4J of the Blue Angels flew aerobatics near Tehran. The names of the Golden Crown pilots are (back row left to right): Imanian, Masoudi, Payadi, Kimiagar, Aghasi Beik, Khalili and Nassikhani.

Aviation Structural Mechanic H (Hydraulics) Airman Elton R. Beck rests on a tow bar attached to a Fighter Squadron 151 F-4S Phantom II aircraft during operations aboard the aircraft carrier USS *Midway* (CV 41).

performance by 50 per cent. The F-4S first flew in May 1958 and set eight new aviation records during its career. Some of those included: altitude (98,557ft), speed (1,390mph), and time to climb (9,000ft in 34.5 seconds). Technically, the leading-edge slats were similar to those fitted to the USAF F-4E, although the outer wing units had a squarer cross-section and had longer wing fences.

The General Electric J-79 engine had lain at the heart of the F-4 Phantom II since the beginning and with the F-4S came the J79-GE-10B version. The F-4 has always been known for its smoking exhaust trails, something that didn't help conceal the aircraft in air-to-air combat with MiGs in Vietnam. Only now, with the advent of the F-4S and this latest version of the J79, were visible smoke emissions reduced through burning JP5s at higher exhaust gas temperatures (EGTs).

Considerable systems' upgrades, following a complete strip down and rebuilding of the chosen airframes, enabled the F-4 to continue operations well into the 1980s. Inevitably, with the entry into service of more modern 'glass cockpit' types and the increasing complexity and challenge of keeping the older F-4S serviceable, the end of F-4 operations for the US Navy and Marine Corps loomed.

Blue Angels US Navy Aerobatic Team

The 'Blues', as the team is known, transitioned to the two-seat McDonnell Douglas F-4J Phantom II in 1968. Interestingly, their aircraft were mostly flown solo with no RIO. In fact, the spare rear seat was useful for demonstration purposes. The Phantom was the only aircraft to be flown by both the 'Blues' and the United States Air Force Thunderbirds (the 'Birds').

The Team's F-4J aircraft were the first twin-engine display aircraft and the Blue Angels performed their first display later in 1968. The display team demonstrated around the world the power of their aircraft and Navy with the added benefit of boosting service morale as well as maintaining public interest in Navy aviation. The Blue Angels used the F-4J for five years with their first South American tour undertaken in 1970. Tours to the Far East followed that took in countries like Japan, South Korea and Taiwan – all locations with a significant US military presence.

The Blue Angels were even decorated, receiving the US Navy's Meritorious Unit Commendation for the period 1 March 1970 to 31 December 1971. The Europeans were not to be denied and so in 1973 the Phantom displays were put on in the UK, Greece, Italy, France, Spain, Turkey and even Iran.

In some ways the F-4J Phantom was an unlikely choice; it was hardly a highly manoeuvrable machine and huge credit must go to the pilots and crews who managed to achieve so much with this heavy, powerful fighter-bomber. The powerful General Electric J79 engines used huge quantities of fuel and, sadly, the team suffered five accidents in the 1969 and 1972/3 seasons and . Further challenges mounted with the international fuel crisis in 1973, so much so that the rest of that season's displays were cancelled. The search was on for a smaller, agile aircraft that was cheaper to run yet offered high levels of manoeuvrability and, after the new LTV A-7 Corsair was discarded, the Blue Angels reformed on the Douglas A-4F Skyhawk.

A British Phantom – United Kingdom

The United Kingdom's Royal Navy was seeking a replacement for the Scimitar and Sea Vixen aircraft that operated from their aircraft carriers. There was much promise that the proposed supersonic P.1154 V/STOL design would be used by the Royal Navy (RN) *and* the Royal Air Force (RAF). The history of what happened next in terms of these home-grown designs is legend and largely depressing to read. Suffice to say that none of the home-grown designs that included the TSR-2 for the RAF came to service with either air arm.

Enter McDonnell Aircraft, who made approaches to Rolls-Royce with proposals for re-engined F-4Bs using that manufacturer's Spey turbofan engine. It was well known that the UK wanted, and arguably needed, high British content in any fleet successor and so their proposals made good business sense. Furthermore, McDonnell Aircraft modified an F-4B in 1963 to accommodate the extendable nose-gear unit that would be needed to launch F-4 aircraft from the British catapults fitted aboard HMS *Ark Royal*.

The Royal Navy placed orders for two prototypes in July 1964, being designated F-4K. As an incentive to order the new F-4K, British manufacturers were offered 50 per cent (later reduced to 40 per cent) of the value of each F-4 in terms of equipment and parts manufacture. Different sections and specifications were split amongst a number of home-based UK manufacturers that included:

- BAC, Preston: aft section of the airframe
- Shorts, Belfast: outer wing sections
- Ferranti: licence-built AN/AWG-10 radar
- Rolls-Royce: Spey turbofan engines
- 30 other UK companies: contracts for various components

The logic for including the Spey seemed strong, with the power plant promising a 25 per cent increase in thrust, reducing take-off distances by one third and increasing savings on fuel consumption. Such alterations would not come cheaply or be easy to achieve with the entire centre

The first Royal Navy Phantom FG.1 (F-4K, serial XT595) landing at the McDonnell Aircraft Corporation, St. Louis, Missouri, USA, on 28 June 1966, the day after its first flight.

A Royal Navy McDonnell Douglas Phantom FG.1 from 892 Naval Air Squadron and a US Navy F-4J Phantom II from Fighter Squadron VF-33 'Tarsiers' about to launch from the aircraft carrier USS *Independence* (CVA-62) in September 1971. The photo was taken during cross-deck operations with the British aircraft carrier HMS *Ark Royal* (R09) during the NATO exercise Royal Knight in the North Atlantic.

A Royal Navy McDonnell Douglas Phantom FG.1 from 892 Naval Air Squadron aboard the aircraft carrier HMS *Ark Royal* (R09). The frigate in the background is either HMS *Tenby* (F65) or HMS *Berwick* (F115).

A 43 Squadron, RAF FG.1 Phantom peels away from her tanker after an in-flight refuelling sortie.

section needing to be widened and deepened to accommodate the Spey engines. The engine intake area was also increased by 20 per cent. Higher exhaust gas temperatures from the Spey engines required greater use of titanium and, overall, these design changes adversely affected the anticipated performance gains from the Spey engines.

On 27 June 1966 the prototype YF-4K lifted off with McDonnell aircraft test pilot Joe Dobronski at the controls. Few issues were encountered and performance was promising during initial test flights with increased fuel consumption and better acceleration at low level. However, at higher altitudes, the F-4J had better performance. Some of the shortcomings in the engine performance were addressed with the Rolls-Royce Spey 202, although it was accepted that the performance compromises were outweighed by F-4 attributes and so development continued apace.

XT897 and XT595 embarked on carrier trials aboard USS *Saratoga*, the former being delivered to the A&AEE Naval Test Squadron at RNAS Yeovilton in 1967.

HMS *Ark Royal* also had to be adapted to take the F-4K; it had to be fitted with water-cooled deck plates and plant deflectors. The F-4K was known by the Royal Navy as the FG.1.

Although originally delivered with the Martin Baker Mk.H5 ejection seats, the FG.1 was later fitted with the more advanced Mk.H7 with zero-zero capability, meaning that aircrew could, in theory, eject safely from ground level. Armament comprised the AIM-7E-2 Sparrow and AIM-9D Sidewinder air-to-air missiles (AAMs). Royal Navy Phantoms were not able to carry an external gun pod (unlike their later RAF cousin, the FGR.2). ML ERU 119 twin-piston ejector release units could carry three 1,000lb bombs.

The Royal Navy was promised 140 FG.1s; however, cost increases and delays led to only 50 airframes being delivered and 20 of these went straight to the RAF. The cost of upgrading HMS *Eagle* to operate the Phantom IIs was rejected, leaving only HMS *Ark Royal* capable of operating the type following an extensive re-fit.

892 Naval Air Squadron operated the FG.1 for nearly ten years. RAF squadrons 111 and 43 also operated the Phantom FG.1.

McDonnell Douglas F-4K Phantom FG.1 of 111 Squadron seen wearing special markings. This aircraft was later scrapped at RAF Wattisham during September 1991. (Mike Freer Collection)

Royal Air Force Phantom FGR.2 and F-4J(UK)

Until perhaps recently, there's never been a great tradition of full co-operation between the Royal Navy and Royal Air Force and this was the case with the procurement of the F-4. The RAF took delivery of 20 FG.1s destined for the Royal Navy and diverted for RAF use. At the time the RAF was less than enthusiastic. Having said that, the cancellation of the RN Hawker Siddeley P.1154 made the project too costly for the RAF to bear alone, leaving only one option: buy a version of the F-4 Phantom II.

It's fair to say that hindsight is a wonderful thing; what the British should have done was buy an off-the-shelf version of the F-4 and had many more aircraft for their money than what transpired. As it was, procurement of the F-4M (the RAF version) would cost as much as the proposed P.1154; each unit cost twice as much as an F-4D and ran overtime. In an ironic twist, the RAF would later require 15 ex-USN F-4Js (designated F-4J(UK) in RAF service) to supplement the RAF air defence fleet ahead of the introduction of the Tornado F.3.

A Royal Air Force F-4J(UK) (RAF serial ZE352, USN BuNo 153783) of 74 Squadron in flight near San Diego, California, USA (27 July 1984) with pilot CDR Steve Queen and RIO Flight-Lieutenant Clive Bairstow. The RAF acquired 15 low-time F-4Js in 1984 and used them until 1991.

The F-4J was arguably better than the FGR.2, although procuring the FGR.2 did provide much needed employment for skilled home-grown workers.

A comparison between the three versions of the F-4 operated by the Royal Navy and Royal Air Force shows a FG.1 with a 100cm (40in) telescopic nose wheel oleo, a hinged nose radome, wider and shorter engine exhausts, bigger air intakes, a deeper rear fuselage, and a radar warning receiver (RWR) installation on the tail fin.

The FGR.2 had no telescopic nose wheel, a fixed nose radome, wider and shorter engine exhausts, bigger air intakes, a deeper rear fuselage, a RWR installation on the tail fin, three small nose gears, and the omission of a bay door light.

The F-4J(UK) had a 51cm (20in) telescopic nose wheel oleo; a fixed nose radome, narrower and longer exhausts, narrower air intakes, a shallower rear fuselage, and no RWR installation on the tail fin.

The RAF bought 118 F-4M aircraft and the type was intended as a multi-role combat aircraft. RAF pilots and navigators were well placed to take on the British variants of the Phantom as many had completed exchange tours with American units and squadrons such as the VMFA-531. Aircraft began to

McDonnell Douglas F-4K Phantom FG.1 of 111 Squadron, RAF Leuchars. This aircraft ended its days at a scrapyard in Glasgow. (Mike Freer)

McDonnell Douglas F-4M Phantom FGR-2 of 92 Squadron, RAF Wildenrath. Later scrapped at RAF Shawbury. (Mike Freer)

McDonnell F-4J(UK) Phantom of 74 Squadron, RAF Wattisham, later issued to the Defence Fire Training & Development Centre at Manston (9083M), was scrapped during 2001. (Mike Freer)

be delivered in the summer of 1968 when XT891 passed through Aldergrove en route to 228 Operational Conversion Unit (OCU) in August that year.

In February 1984 the UK Air Defence Region needed a boost so the RAF purchased 15 former US Navy F-4Js with low flying hours. This was as a result of a squadron of RAF Phantoms being deployed to the Falkland Islands during that conflict in 1982. Following the war 1435 Flight provided an air defence unit at Stanley airfield (Falkland Islands). The Flight reformed with Hawker Siddeley Harrier GR.3 aircraft in late 1983 as the unit had been badly damaged during the fighting – it was disbanded in May 1985. In November 1988, when 23 Squadron converted to the Tornado, 1435 Flight was revived and equipped with four McDonnell Douglas Phantom FGR.2s. After 23 Squadron's disbandment at RAF Mount Pleasant the mission and equipment were transferred to 1435 Flight. The Phantoms were replaced in July 1992 when four Panavia Tornado F3s arrived in the Falklands. The Flight was later re-equipped with the Eurofighter Typhoon FGR.4 and maintains a 365-day, 24-hour alert capability.

The F-4J(UK) was a very cost-effective solution until the Tornado F.3 entered service. Because the aircraft in RAF service were a special production batch, built to UK specifications, it would not be possible to obtain identical aircraft. Thus the 15 airframes were procured from among the best of the former USN F-4Js stored at the Aerospace Maintenance and Regeneration Center at Davis–Monthan Air Force Base in Arizona. The selected airframes were extensively refurbished and

FGR-2 XV420 56 Squadron seen at RAF Mildenhall Air Fete, 1990. Note that at that stage the green-grey camouflage over light aircraft grey (LAG) had been replaced with barley grey upper surfaces over LAG undersides.

Left and below: Phantom FGR.2s operating towards the end of their service with 19 and 92 squadrons in Germany at RAF Wildenrath looked incredibly worn as can be seen here with these two fantastic photographs. (Ian Black)

brought to a standard almost equivalent to the F-4S, which was the last variant in service with the USN, the only differences being the absence of leading-edge slats and a helmet gun sight. The leading-edge slats were omitted partly on grounds of cost but also because the RAF liked the additional speed a hard-wing offered combat crews.

The F-4J was chosen because it was the variant from which the RAF's F-4Ks (FGR.2) and F-4Ms (FG.1) had been developed, and was thus the closest available to the British aircraft.

The RAF favoured the SUU-23A gun pod so the 'new' F-4Js were wired to accommodate the gun pod and Sky Flash AAMs. The radar was upgraded to AN/AWG-10B standard. Although initially supplied with the US Navy Martin Baker MB Mk.H7 ejector seats, these were later replaced with Mk.7A-4s from surplus FG.1s.

The major difference between the F-4J and the British Phantoms was the absence of the Rolls-Royce Spey turbofan, the former being fitted with the General Electric J79-10B turbojet. Initially capable of carrying the AIM-7 Sparrow and AIM-9 Sidewinder air-to-air missiles (AAM), they were soon made compatible with the Skyflash and SUU-23A gun pod, bringing them into line with the rest of the RAF's Phantoms. Despite modifications to allow them to operate with the rest of the fleet, the F-4Js retained the vast bulk of the equipment they were originally fitted with, even requiring their crews to use American flying helmets.

Although the new Phantoms were assigned the F.3 British designation, they were generally referred to as the F-4J(UK). They were assigned to 74 Squadron at RAF Wattisham, which stood up in October 1984, two months after the first flight. The aircraft remained in service through the transition to the Tornado F2/3, which began entering service in 1987. In 1990, thanks to the conversion of FGR.2 squadrons to the Tornado, the RAF was able to transfer the best of its remaining FGR.2s to 74 Squadron. This meant that the F.3

RAF Phantom FGR.2s when on battle flight alert carried four AIM-9L Sidewinder and AIM-7 Sparrow/Skyflash air-to-air missiles (AAMs) and the SUU-23A Vulcan Rotary cannon (shown here) on the centreline hardpoint. Note the heavy staining on the underside of the fuselage that was typical of operational FGR.2s in the 1980s.

The 74 (Fighter) 'Tiger' Squadron unit badge applied to Phantom FGR.2 XV474 'T' 74. The 'Tigers' operated FGR.2s towards the end of their RAF service. 74 (Fighter) 'Tiger' Squadron was reformed after being dormant for 13 years, reforming at RAF Wattisham, Suffolk, on 19 October 1984.

F-4J(UK) ZE361 seen at RAF Wyton open day in 1988.

ZE351 (I), F-4J(UK), RAF Finningley, September 1988. (Derek Bradshaw)

Three US Navy McDonnell F-4J Phantom IIs (BuNo s155574, 155825, 157290) from Fighter Squadron 103 (VF-103) 'Sluggers' in flight. VF-103 was assigned to Carrier Air Wing 3 (CVW-3) aboard the aircraft carrier USS *Saratoga* (CV-60) for a deployment to the Mediterranean Sea from 6 January to 28 July 1976.

was able to be withdrawn in January 1991. With a couple of exceptions, all the RAF's F-4Js were broken up for scrap. One of the 15 airframes was lost in a crash in 1987, killing both crew members.

In the UK, the British Phantom Aviation Group is working hard to restore airframe F-4J(UK) ZE360 to a high-quality static exhibit which will be the only surviving example that will commemorate the significant contribution and sacrifice made by all involved in the 15 aircraft operated by the RAF's 74 'Tiger' Squadron.

ZE360 began its life as F-4J BuNo 155574 at McDonnell Douglas's Lambert Field facility in St. Louis, USA. Its maiden flight was on 6 April 1968 and it was subsequently accepted by the US Navy on 9 April, then issued to Fighter Squadron VF-31 'Tomcatters' on 22 May. Over the next 13 years it was based primarily on the east coast of the USA, its shore home being NAS Oceana, Virginia. It served aboard the USS *Franklin D. Roosevelt*, *Independence* and *Saratoga*, embarking on cruises of the Atlantic and Mediterranean. Time was also spent with other units, including VF-41 'Black Aces', VF-101 'Grim Reapers' and VF-103 'Sluggers' before ending its days in US service with a Marine Corps squadron: VMFAT-101 'Sharpshooters' at Marine Corps Air Station Yuma, Arizona in August 1981. Some of the US inventory of F-4Js were scheduled to be upgraded to the new F-4S standard but the rest were moved into storage. In the case of ZE360 this was at North Island, California, and the story might have finished there were it not for the UK's victory in the Falklands conflict in June 1982.

F-4J(UK) Phantom ZE360 can be seen in its original livery when operated by Fighter Squadron 103 (VF-103) 'Sluggers' in 1976.

United States Air Force: F-4C

United States Air Force (USAF) use of the F-4 dates back to the beginning of 1962 when they received a couple of F-4H-1s from US Navy stock. Incredibly, the USAF would go on to operate a total of just over 2,900 F-4s in a number of variants. In November 1963 the US Air Force received steady deliveries of the F-4C model. The F-4C had a lot in common with its US Navy counterpart, the F-4B, with only relatively small changes that included thicker main gear tyres and an anti-skid system which led to a slightly thicker wing root. In-flight refuelling was taken care of by moving the retractable probe (IFR) from the starboard side of the forward fuselage to a dorsal receptacle on the spine just behind the cockpit. There was no need for the catapult bridle horns used on US Navy Phantoms and located just under the front wing roots, thus they were removed on the F-4C.

The F-4C was a complex machine and a significant step-up from the aircraft it replaced; this inevitably led aircrew to either love it for its strengths or desire changes. Given the immersion of US forces in Vietnam, these developments, modifications and upgrades needed to be incorporated quickly which led to a rather random layout

Left: A Hawaii Air National Guard F-4C Phantom II aircraft deploys a drogue chute during a landing.

Below: A right front view of an F-4C Phantom II aircraft loaded with a camera pod, Eglin Air Force Base.

of boxes, displays and other equipment in the cockpits for the pilot and RIO.

By the end of 1965 the F-4C was well established in South East Asia, equipping 6 squadrons, rising to 12 within the next 18 months.

SMART weapons hadn't really entered service when one compares the munitions available at the time with what is on offer today. Loads typically comprised six 500lb Mk.82 Snakeyes, or low-drag fragmentation bombs, or six higher-capacity M117 750lb bombs and unpinned BLU-1/B or -27/B napalm tanks, CBU-24/B CBUs, LAU-3 or 61 2.75in FFAR rocket pods and occasionally, AGM-12B Bullpup radio-controlled missiles.

The SUU-16/A gun pod was popular in Vietnam and began to be fitted to the F-4C around 1967, a year that also heralded the introduction into service and combat in Vietnam of the F-4Cs successor, the F-4D.

USAF: F-4D

The F-4D was equipped with SUU-16/A gun pod connectivity and was able to carry the later and more capable SUU-23/A version of this impressive air-to-air gun.

The F-4D was almost identical to the F-4C to look at, although this disguised the fact that the model was a far more capable fighting machine and differed greatly under the skin, mainly because it was the first USAF Phantom variant that incorporated all the modifications that the Air Force really wanted. It entered service in December 1965 and was the first F-4 variant to be optimized for ground attack sorties.

The F-4D retained the same basic airframe design as the F-4C and same engines, thus retaining the same fuel capacity of the RF-4C. Perhaps the major differences lay in the avionics with the APQ-100 being replaced by the smaller, smarter AN/APA-65 radar unit that introduced an air-to-ground ranging mode. The type was capable of delivering LGBs (Laser Guided Bombs) and other 'smart' weapons with the back-seater (RIO) being given a television display that assisted in the delivery of GBU-8 (initially) and later GBU-15 ordnance. Unguided weapons like the Mk.82 500-lb Snakeye were commonly carried in air-to-ground missions.

Major Michael R. Caan, an engineering pilot, and British Royal Air Force Captain Batt aboard an F-4C Phantom II aircraft. Here, Major Caan is assigned to the 110th Tactical Fighter Squadron, 131st Tactical Fighter Wing, Missouri Air National Guard, involved in Exercise Coronet Cactus, RAF Leeming, Yorkshire, UK. Even as late as the mid-1980s there were F-4C visitors to the UK, sporting their glossy light-grey camouflage.

Apart from the modifications already mentioned, the F-4D could be readily identified externally by the large AN/ARN-92 LORAN navigation receiver on the upper centre fuselage, although this was not fitted to all F-4D aircraft. Additionally, small RHAW sensors were fitted to the tail cone/brake chute housing. An AN-APS-107A RHAW Antenna was fitted to the top aft section of the fin. Externally hung

Two photos showing F-4C 40707 visiting RAF Mildenhall Air Fete.

A US Air Force McDonnell F-4D Phantom II aircraft from the 8th Tactical Fighter Wing, Kunsan Air Base, South Korea, in flight on 1 April 1980. The aircraft is equipped with a GBU-12D 227kg laser-guided bomb, an AN/ALQ-119 electronic countermeasures pod, a Pave Spike laser designator, and a SUU-16/A 20mm gun pod.

Two US Air Force McDonnell F-4D-30-MC Phantom II fighters (s/n 66-7576, 66-7628) from the 435th Tactical Fighter Squadron, 8th Tactical Fighter Wing, over Vietnam, off the wing of a Boeing KC-135A Stratotanker. Both Phantoms are armed with three SUU-30/B cluster bombs (right wing), three LAU-3 rocket launchers (left wing) and six Mk.82 227kg bombs (centreline). F-4D 66-7576 was written off in Vietnam on 30 July 1972.

electronic jammers included ALQ-87, ALQ-101 and ALQ-119. A Multiple Ejector Rack (MER) could be fitted to the centreline stores station beneath the aircraft, a location that had originally been intended for a fuel tank. Triple Ejector racks (TERs) for bombs could be carried on the inboard and underwing pylons.

The F-4Ds began to enter service in March 1966, going to the 36th Tactical Fighter Wing (TFW) based at Bitburg, Germany. Then in January 1967 the 4th TFW took delivery of their F-4Ds while based at Seymour Johnson AFB, North Carolina. With the F-4C already committed to operations in Vietnam, the earlier designation began to be replaced by the F-4D from spring 1967. Interestingly, this was with Lieutenant-Colonel Robin Olds, 8th TFW, 'Wolfpack'.

There was controversy when the F-4D said goodbye to the AIM-9B AAM in favour of the AIM-4D Falcon. Aircraft could carry four of these Mach 3 missiles; however, their performance was disappointing.

The AIM-4's poor kill record rendered the F-4 ineffective in air-to-air combat; the fighters were modified to carry the USN-designed AIM-9 Sidewinder missile instead, which was already carried on USN and USMC F-4 Phantom IIs and F-8 Crusader jet fighters. The Sidewinder was

Staff Sergeant Jerry Stanton, a 924th Tactical Fighter Group crew chief, greets Major Rick Coneway and Major Dale Fiala as they climb out of their F-4D Phantom II aircraft during Exercise Team Spirit 1985, Kunsan Air Base.

Left: A left front view of an F-4D Phantom II aircraft parked on the flight line. The Phantom is equipped with a camera pod on the left wing and a Pave Spike laser target designator pod on the fuselage, Eglin Air Force Base.

Below: AIM-4 Falcon at Hill Air Force Base.

Centre and bottom: A view of the radar system of an F-4D Phantom II aircraft, as it undergoes repairs during Exercise Coronet Brave, RAF Finningley.

much more effective and improved versions continue to serve the armed forces of the United States and numerous allied nations to this day. A further issue with the AIM-4 was that it wasn't fitted with a proximity fuse, meaning that you had to score a direct hit to land a kill.

USAF: Enter the F-4E

No fewer than 865 F-4Es equipped US Air Force squadrons over the nine years of operations from 1967 to December 1976 and the type's outstanding performance led directly to sales success of the type overseas, with many air forces ultimately operating the type.

The Thunderbirds' aerial demonstration squadron (ADS) wore the eye-catching red-white-and-blue stars and stripes ensuring the team were instantly recognizable wherever they were deployed around the world and the performances undoubtedly contributed to the success of the F-4E variant.

On operational deployment, the F-4E was bulkier and looked incredibly business-like, sporting the 'Lizard' South East Asia (SEA) paint scheme. The F-4E was also the heaviest version of the Phantom to see service. October 1967 saw the F-4E enter US service, although this was anything but smooth. Problems arose with the Hughes Coherent On Receiver Doppler Sub-System (CORDS), a key component of the F-4E's airborne missile and control system. (ACMS). The system was designed, in part, to be able to identify low-flying MiGs from the ground clutter. CORDS was abandoned in January 1968.

A Westinghouse AN/APQ-120(V) fire control system lay at the heart of the F-4E's radar package and was designed to fit inside the tapered, more slim-line nose cone, arguably making this the most aesthetic version of the famous Phantom II.

Problems continued as a result of vibrations caused by firing the immense

An air-to-air left front view of an F-4E Phantom II aircraft (top) and an F-4G Wild Weasel Phantom II aircraft (bottom). Note the open refuelling port on the top of the F-4E. Both aircraft are equipped with AN/ALQ-119 electronic countermeasure pods. They are assigned to the 3rd Tactical Fighter Wing, Clark Air Base, Philippines.

A profile view of the left side of an F-4E Phantom II aircraft (foreground) and a F-5E Tiger II aircraft.

Front view of an F-4E Phantom II aircraft assigned to the 474th Tactical Training Wing, parked on the apron, Nellis Air Force Base.

GE Vulcan rotary cannon while the exhaust gases also caused a number of engine flameouts. Eventually, of course, the engineers found a solution in the Midas IV gun shroud where the louvres diverted the gasses out of and under the belly of the aircraft. A buffer-proof mounting for the gun was added that helped prevent vibrations and adverse effects on the radar.

New engines were also fitted to the F-4E, namely the General Electric J79-GE-17 that packed a punch of 11,870lb static thrust per engine at full military power and 17,900lb static thrust in reheat. A slotted all-moving tailplane, originally developed for the US Navy F-4J, was also fitted. The aim of the slotted stabilizer, with inverted aerofoil leading edge, was to provide a more positive pitch response and at lower speeds like during landings.

By November 1967 F-4Es provided USAF squadrons with its first operational unit: the 33rd Fighter Wing based at Eglin AFB, Florida. The first F-4Es to be deployed to South East Asia were the 4th, 16th and 40th squadrons. They deployed to the 388th Fighter Wing based at Korat, Royal Thai AFB, Thailand, in November 1967. This is where the menacing-looking shark mouths were applied – a trademark of the squadron. 1 January 1969 saw the first loss of an F-4E and it wouldn't be the last. A total of 73 F-4Es would go down before hostilities ceased in Vietnam.

F-4Es sported some excellent names, such as Betty Lou (the subject of a scale model build in this book); Arizona Chicken (66-371) and The Wreckin Crew (70-279) 34th Fighter Wing.

The F-4E bred a new type of aircrew with a pilot and backseat pilot/weapons systems officer (P-WSOs). Prior to this two fully qualified pilots crewed the aircraft. Now there was a genuine team that involved the pilot flying the aircraft and the P-WSO spending most of his time managing the weapons, systems and navigation. The F-4 community finally departed Thailand in summer 1974.

F-4 in Foreign Service

Australia

The F-4C variant of the Phantom II was among the aircraft evaluated by the RAAF in 1963 as part of a project to replace its English Electric Canberra bombers. The F-111 was selected, but when that project was delayed in the late 1960s due to long-running technical faults with the aircraft, the RAAF determined that the F-4E Phantom II would be the best alternative. As a result of continued problems with the F-111s, the Australian and United States governments negotiated an agreement in 1970 whereby the RAAF leased 24 F-4Es and their support equipment from the USAF. The project was named 'Peace Reef'. The contract was signed on 22 June 1970 and the first of the F-4Es arrived the following September. They served with 1 and 6 squadrons, both based at Royal Australian AFB Amberley. The RAAF operated the 24 Phantoms in the ground-attack role between 1970 and 1973. Used in their intended air-to-ground role, they prepared aircrew to operate the sophisticated F-111s, and the intensive training programme undertaken using the aircraft improved the RAAF's professional standards. One of the Phantoms was destroyed in a flying accident in June 1971, and another was repaired by the RAAF after it sustained heavy damage during a crash landing. Although the F-4Es were considered successful in their role, the government did not agree to a proposal from the RAAF to retain the aircraft after the F-111s entered service in 1973.

The first six F-4E aircraft were returned in October 1972 and the first six F-111Cs were delivered in June 1973; the rest of the F-4Es were returned to the United States Air Force later that month.

Egypt

Egypt received 36 F-4Es under the Peace Pharaoh project as a sign of goodwill from the Americans for signing the Camp David Accords. The Accords, signed by President Jimmy Carter, Egyptian President Anwar Sadat and Israeli Prime Minister Menachem Begin in September 1978, established a framework for an historic peace treaty concluded between Israel and Egypt on 29 March 1979. With the signing of the treaty, Egypt ended its military dependence on the Soviet Union. It also lost the financial support of the other Arab states, and Saudi Arabia cancelled its plans to send Egypt 50 F-5s. The US State Department proposed trading Egypt new military hardware in exchange for military

Royal Australian Air Force McDonnell Douglas F-4E Phantom II at Edinburgh, South Australia, 1971. (Chris Finney)

A profile view of the right side of an Egyptian air force McDonnell Douglas F-4E Phantom II aircraft in formation with a 347th Tactical Fighter Wing F-4E aircraft during exercise Proud Phantom in 1980.

aircraft made in the USSR, including MiG-21s and the newer MiG-23s, delivered to them by the Soviets prior to their breakdown of relations in 1976. The first batch of 18 fighters arrived in Egypt in October 1979. The Egyptian Phantoms were ex-USAF aircraft previously flown by the 31st Fighter Wing based at Homestead AFB. They were initially operated by 76 and 88 squadrons of the 222nd Fighter Regiment, Egyptian Air Force (Al Quwwat al Jawwiya il Misriya).

In addition to the F-4E aircraft, various munitions were supplied that included a number of AIM-7 Sparrow, AIM-9 Sidewinder and AGM-65 Maverick missiles going to the Egyptian Air Force for US$594 million. Initially, Egyptian ground crews found their maintenance far more complex than that required for Soviet aircraft and consequently there was an average of only nine F-4s serviceable during 1982, a 26 per cent serviceability rate. To correct the situation Egypt considered selling some of the F-4s to Turkey and buying extra General Dynamics F-16 Fighting Falcons. However, assistance from US advisors in 1985 made it possible to reach a reasonable serviceability rate, and in 1988 another seven F-4s were delivered. While further purchases of F-4s and upgrades were considered, these plans were rejected in favour of additional orders for F-16s.

By the end of the 1990s, three aircraft had crashed but were replaced. In 2018 the two F-4 squadrons were retired and are in storage/reserve.

Germany

The German Air Force was one of the biggest F-4 customers outside the US, operating a total of 175 F-4Fs, 10 F-4Es (for training at US airfields) and 88 RF-4Es.

The RF-4E was the first F-4 model to enter German service. The German Air Force signed a contract with McDonnell Douglas for 88 RF-4Es in 1968. The contract was attractive to Germany as it included industrial offsets for German industry, particularly production work for Messerschmitt-Bölkow-Blohm who manufactured and supplied F-4 components to McDonnell Douglas's Phantom production facility in St. Louis.

Under the Peace Rhine modification programme, the German Air Force purchased the F-4F, which was based on the F-4E. The F-4F had one of the seven fuselage fuel tanks omitted along with the capability to carry AIM-7 Sparrow missiles and bombs. It was equipped with air combat manoeuvring leading-edge slats and had a higher thrust-to-weight ratio, approaching 1:1 when fuel was low.

F-4Fs equipped a number of German Air Force units that included Jagdgeschwader (JG) 74 'Mölders'. In April 1975, deliveries started to Jagdbombergeschwader (JaboG) 36, Rheine-Hopsten Air Base and to JaboG 35, Pferdsfeld Air Base. Operationally, the F-4Fs used by JG.71 and JG.74 were employed in the air-to-air role, while those used by JaboG 35 and 36 were also used in air-to-ground roles.

At the end of their service, German Air Force F-4Fs sported some amazingly colourful schemes that appeal to many, not least scale modellers, many of whom love to finish their aircraft in such schemes.

Ahead of the introduction of the four-nation European Fighter Aircraft (EFA) that was to become Eurofighter, Germany decided to upgrade its fleet of F-4s that

A pair of German McDonnell Douglas F-4F Phantoms after receiving fuel. The F-4Fs are from Jagdgeschwader 74 (JG 74) based at Neuburg, Bavaria, Germany, and the KC-135R was from the 100th Aerial Refuelling Wing, Royal Air Force, Mildenhall, UK.

German Air Force F-4F 37 + 03 of Jagdgeschwader 71 'Richthofen', Wittmund, 2009. (Leo Kiewik)

F-4F Phantom II 'Black Beauty' of the former JG 72 'Westfalen' and later F-4F flight training centre after the unit's last flight. Located at Wittmund Air Base. (Jens Schleck www.etnp.de)

Hellenic Air Force F-4E. Note the heavy weathering, especially on the starboard wing drop tank. (Leo Kiewik)

would see their service lives extended to 2005.

Late 1983 saw the introduction of the ICE (Improved Combat Efficiency) programme which upgraded the F-4F's air-to-air capabilities. This involved the APG-65 radar and AIM-120 AMRAAM as the main elements, along with many minor upgrades. The original plan was to upgrade 75 F-4Fs, but the number was increased to 110 in the late 1980s. Initially, the ICE upgrades were intended only for the interceptor wings, but more were upgraded due to delays in the Eurofighter.

At the heart of the F-4F ICE capability was the APG-65 radar that was originally used by the F/A-18 Hornet operating with multiple air arms across the globe. Although superseded in performance by the APG-73, the original unit remained the standard against which others were measured. Furthermore, the Hughes AIM-120 AMRAAM (Advanced Medium Range Air-to-Air Missile) relies on a type of semi-active radar homing at range for the initial part of its flight. The target must be illuminated by the launch aircraft with the missile taking over mid-range internal guidance and final closure to impact; therefore the missile has an element of fire-and-forget capability. When in closer engagements, the AIM-120 can handle homing on its own.

In September 1991, three aircraft were deployed to the NAWC Weapons Division at Point Mugu for evaluation and the launch of six instrumented AMRAAMs was proposed. The first of these took place on 22 November 1991 with the successful destruction of the target drone. This was significant, marking the first launch of an AMRAAM by a foreign aircraft. By July 1992, six ICE-converted aircraft had been delivered to JG.71 'Richthofen'. The German Air Force retired their F-4Fs on 29 June 2013.

Greece

1974 saw the introduction of the first 18 F-4E Phantom IIs into the Hellenic Air Force (Polemikí Aeroporía), partially funded by US military assistance as part of Operation Icarus. A second batch of F-4Es, plus two extra aircraft, were delivered in 1976, followed by a final batch in 1978–79.

The first units equipped were the 339th Squadron in 1974 in the air-to-air role as well as an operational training unit and the 338th Squadron, in 1975, in the ground-attack role. The 337th 'Ghost' Squadron was equipped in 1978, giving up their Northrop F-5As. The 348th 'Eyes' Squadron relinquished their RF-84Fs for new RF-4Es in 1979. The old RF-84Fs were retained until 1990 for training purposes.

The last batch of 40 Phantoms was not delivered due to the political instability in Greece; the Iraqi invasion of Kuwait and the US-led Operation Desert Storm reversed that short delivery. The USAF phased out many older aircraft, supplying some to the PA as a token of gratitude for the use of Greek air bases during the war. These included 10 former Indiana Air National Guard aircraft and were later followed by another 18 aircraft.

By 1992 there were 4 squadrons equipped with 73 F-4Es and 5 RF-4Es: these were the 348th and 337th squadrons in Larissa with the 110th Combat Wing, and the 338th and 339th squadrons at Andravida with the 117th Combat Wing.

There were many differences between the batches supplied to the Hellenic Air Force. The 338th 'Ares' Squadron had an air-to-surface role. Their F-4Es were equipped with digital processors for the APG-120, laser inertial navigation systems, digital data buses, smoke-reduction systems and various structural improvements.

The 339th 'Ajax' Squadron was employed in the air-defence role with the older Phantoms, which had a Radar Warning Receiver mounted on the tail and air intakes, as well as a TISEO (Target Identification System Electro-Optical) optical device. Interceptors can be armed with AIM-7E Sparrow, AIM-120 AMRAAM and AIM-9 Sidewinder AAMs and have exchanged their two-tone green and brown camouflage for a bluish-grey and light grey pattern. (Colours: 36307, 36251, 35237 and 36320).

Greek F-4E Phantoms (PI2000) continue in service and are used in the interception, fighter-bomber and reconnaissance roles.

Iran

Other export customers followed with a huge order of 177 F-4Es, plus 32 F-4Ds, in September 1968 from Iran, with F-4E deliveries to the Imperial Iranian Air Force (IIAF) commencing in March 1971 through to August 1979 and RF-4s from February 1971. In total, the 225 Phantoms delivered gave the IIAF over 12 squadrons. Those tasked with interception were armed with AIM-7E Sparrow AAMs and AIM-9J Sidewinder AAMs. They first saw action in the ground-attack role in 1975 when Iran provided assistance to the Sultan of Oman to tackle rebel forces in the Dhofar region.

Iran's first aircraft were initially assigned to the 306th Fighter Squadron and, in fact, only one other unit was equipped before the arrival of the F-4E in much greater numbers; these F-4Es are still active today. The F-4Ds were issued with local serial numbers, beginning 3-601, 3-602, and so on.

In September 1980 when Iraq attacked Iran, the IIAF had 190 Phantoms on charge, although only around 40 per cent were serviceable due to a lack of spares brought about by a US embargo. Losses were high during the first nine months

All below: Hellenic Air Force RF-4E Phantom II, Tanagra Air Base, Greece, during Athens Flying Week Air Show in 2018. (Derek Bradshaw)

Above: An IIAF F-4E Phantom II departs its base. (Shahram Sharifi)

Israeli Air Force 201 Squadron F-4E Phantom II at Tel Nof, Independence Day 2013. (Oren Rozen)

with 60 F-4s being lost and many aircraft remaining grounded due to a lack of spares. Secretly, Israel supplied some spares and others were obtained from various sources worldwide. Politics being what it is, the US broke its own embargo during 1985/6 in what became known as the 'Irangate' scandal. By August 1988, it was estimated that only around a maximum of 30 F-4s remained operational. Tensions continued in the region, not least with Saudi Arabia that operated the F-15C Eagle and during a border skirmish one IIAF F-4E was downed.

Israel

The US Foreign Military Sales (FMS) programme handled overseas sales of the Phantom II and the launch customer for the FMSs F-4Es was the Israel Defense Forces' Air Force (IDF/AF). They ordered 50 Phantoms (44 F-4E and 6 RF-4Es) in a deal that was announced in December 1968.

Ten Israeli aircrew, including four navigators, began training at George AFB, California with the 4452nd TFTS in March 1969 and graduated at the end of July. The Israel Defense Forces/Air Force received its first aircraft in September 1969. The original F-4Es were delivered initially by US Air Force and later McDonnell aircrews at a rate of four per month until November 1972. These aircraft were not fitted with leading-edge slats nor AXS-1 TISEO. TISEO is an auto daytime passive target acquisition and tracking sensor using closed-circuit television with optics offering two magnifications, and is located in a pod on the left wing leading edge.

IDF F-4E Phantoms were in action on 22 October 1969 when they struck SA-2 SAM sites near Port Said, Egypt. The IDF strategy was to make supersonic flypasts over Cairo to instil panic and further destabilize the country.

Encounters between Egyptian MiG-21s were common in the late 1960s and on 2 April 1969 an Israeli F-4E was shot down by a MiG-21 and the crew taken prisoner. Another F-4E was lost to mechanical failure but its crew ejected over Israel. Problems continued to mount for Israeli F-4Es as Egypt began to move its SAM (surface-to-air) missile sites closer to the Suez Canal and losses mounted for the Israeli Air Force. This period became known as the War of Attrition and ended with a ceasefire on 7 August 1971.

The Yom Kippur War in 1973 took a heavy toll on the IDF/AF. Of the 11,233 IDF/AF combat sorties of all types, 37 Phantoms were lost and 6 more severely damaged and deemed beyond repair.

Inevitably, given the damage incurred by the Phantom fleet, there was an urgent need to repair and upgrade the airframes. This opportunity was taken by adding a new radar warning receiver, leading-edge slats and TISEO to the existing early aircraft. Numerous upgrades have been conducted since and this has naturally led to Israeli F-4s with different specifications. Most had a new Elbit Jason digital weapons delivery/navigational system and some have external in-flight refuelling (IFR) probes.

In the late 1970s the IDF/AF re-equipment plans were somewhat overambitious; the replacement of the A-4 Skyhawk and Kfir by the IAI Lavi would leave insufficient funds for an F-4 replacement that they hoped would be the F/A-18 Hornet. This led directly to the Kurnass 2000 update programme where the F-4 was equipped with new engines and avionics suites. The planned programme to replace the original J79 engines with the Pratt & Whitney PW1120 was cancelled but the fleet was updated to Kurnass 2000 standards. This upgrade included the installation of a wide-angle Kaiser HUD, a digital mission computer as well as some structural improvements. The main updates involved the APG-76 radar, Elbit ACE-3 mission computer, HOTAS, the addition of winglets for increased agility, ASX-1 TISEO and the ability to deploy Popeye missiles. The upgraded aircraft first flew on 15 July 1987 and was formally accepted on 11 August 1987. The Kurnass programme was also used to upgrade Turkish Air Force Phantoms at the same time, realizing some economies of scale.

By the end of the 20th century there were still 112 F-4s serving with the IDF, in three Squadrons: 119, 142 and 201. Israeli Phantoms have suffered at least 55 combat losses but accounted for 116.5 air victories.

A ground-to-air left underside view of two Mitsubishi-built F-4EJ Phantom II aircraft of the Japan Air Self-Defense Force (JASDF) in formation during joint US Air Force and JASDF Exercise Cope North.

Naval Air Facility Misawa, Japan, 8 September 2002. A pair of Japanese Air Self-Defense Force (JASDF) F-4 Phantoms take off from one of the runways on the Misawa Air Base during their annual air festival. (US Navy)

M131 (Mitsubishi built) operated by the Air Development & Test Wing (AD&TW), Japanese Air Self-Defence Force, Gifu Air Base, 15th March 2019.

Japan

McDonnell Aircraft supplied 2 new-build F-4EJ Phantoms and a further 11 in kit form for assembly in Japan. Japan would go on to produce 127 additional aircraft for the Japan Air Self-Defense Force (Nihon Koku Jietai). The first home-assembled F-4EJ (s/n 27-8303) took to the air on 12 May 1972.

Although initial deliveries were assigned to the Air Proving Wing at Gifu, there were soon sufficient aircraft to allow for the 1st Hikotai, 301 'The Frogs' Tactical Fighting Squadron, on 16 October 1973.

1984 saw the first flight of the advanced F-4EJ Kai (*Kai* meaning extra or augmented), the result of a challenging Service Life Extension Programme (SLEP) that would equip the JASDF with a highly capable fighter into the 1990s and beyond. The first operational F-4EJ Kai entered service on 24 November 1990 and, incredibly, the last of the type were retired at the end of 2020.

The primary intention of the Kai programme was to extend the service life of each aircraft from 3,000 to 5,000 hours. The Kai featured multiple upgrades and additions that included AN/APG-66J pulse-Doppler radar that featured a better look-down/shoot-down capability, Kaiser HUD, Hazeltine AN/APZ-79A IFF system and licence-built Litton LN-39.

Some, believed to be around 29, of the F-4EJs were converted to the reconnaissance role as RF-4EJ Kai.

F-4Js were delivered in a livery of light grey upper surfaces and white undersides; this gave way to experimental schemes with blue and/or grey medium altitude camouflage, beginning in 1979. RF-4E aircraft arrived in light grey and white and moved to two-tone green and tan in 1977. In the years since their introduction the JASDF F-4EJ and EJ Kai aircraft have sported some of the most spectacular colour schemes ever applied to military aircraft anywhere in the world.

301 Hikotai's two retirement schemes were applied to F-4EJ Kais 37-8315 and 07-8436. The first scheme was applied before the Hyakuri Phantom Phinale air festival in November 2019 to 37-8315. This scheme saw a yellow shark mouth applied to the nose with yellow and black bands on the wings, fuselage and external fuel tanks; the squadron's insignia of a Japanese frog on the tail fin. 'Go for it!! 301sq' was adorned on the air intakes. The squadron's frog logo, as applied spectacularly to the tail of 37-8315, was adopted in 1974 and is in homage to the frogs of Mount Tsukuba close to Hyakuri Air Base. The seven stars on the frog's scarf denote that the Hikotai belonged to the 7th Air Wing in Hyakuri. The frog now wears three stars on its scarf since its move to JASDF Misawa as it currently operates under the 3rd Air Wing.

Appearing in the summer of 2020, the second aircraft, 07-8436, also had a shark's mouth applied and a striking blue, white and black scheme on the fuselage, wings and external fuel tanks. Fittingly, a phantom spook was applied to the tail fin whilst 'Thank you Phantom II' was applied to the upper wing surface and 'Phantom Forever' to the aircraft's air intakes. A nice touch on the intake splitter plates are the logos of all JASDF squadrons that operated the F-4EJ or RF-4EJ. One of 301 Hikotai's F-4EJ Kai aircraft, 17-8440, aka 'Shishumaru', is one of the few that has been chosen to be preserved. This aircraft is of historical interest as it was the very last Phantom of the 5,195 to be built. It was delivered to the JASDF on 20 May 1981 and took its final flight late that November from JASDF Hyakuri to JASDF Hammamatsu where it went on display at the impressive air museum.

South Korea

The Peace Spectator programme saw the delivery of 18 former USAF F-4Ds to South Korea. They served with the 110th Tactical Fighter Squadron, 11th Fighter Wing, based at Daegu. In 1972 another 18 were delivered from the USAF 3rd Tactical Fighter Wing, in exchange for which South Korea delivered 36 Northrop F-5As to South Vietnam. Several more F-4s were delivered in the following years, with the last batch delivered during 1987 and 1988. These were equipped with Pave Tack laser designators, an important feature that allowed the use of laser-guided bombs.

A total of 92 F-4Ds were delivered, making this air force the main export customer for the F-4D model. The F-4Ds were joined by 37 new-build F-4Es, ordered in the 1970s. The last of these was the 5,068th F-4 built in St. Louis. Under Operation Peace Pheasant these were delivered to the Republic of Korea Air Force's (RoKAF) 152 and 153 Tactical Fighter Squadrons, 17th Tactical Fighter Wing, Chongju. This was only the beginning of South Korean F-4 acquisitions, as more ex-USAF F-4Es were delivered over the next few years, eventually totalling 103 F-4Es.

Overall, South Korea was one of the main customers of the F-4, with 216 delivered, including 60 F-4D models, 55 F-4E models and 18 RF-4Cs in service in 2000.

Spain

Spain needed a replacement for its F-104G Starfighter and North American F-86F Sabre aircraft in 1971 that made up their frontline ADF (Air Defence Force. Under the Mutual Defense Aid Programme (MDAP) Spain received 36 former USAF F-4Cs for its Air Force (*Ejército del Aire*). The F-4Cs came from the USAF's 81st TFW at Bentwaters, England and received an overhaul by CASA at Getafe before being handed over to the EdA. Interestingly, these were the only F-4C models ever exported, even as second-hand examples. During their service, seven F-4Cs were lost to accidents before being replaced by EF-18s in April 1989.

Top and above: F-4EJ Kai 07-8436. (Emil Cooper)

Further F-4 deliveries took place in October 1978 with the addition of four F-4Cs and four-RF-4Cs. The RF-4Cs were given the Spanish designation CR.12. In fact, eight RF-4Cs were supplied from the 123rd TRW (Tactical Reconnaissance Wing), Kentucky ANG, the first six arriving at Torrejon on 11 January 1989. These aircraft formed a new squadron, 123 Escuadron (Callsign 'Titan') within Ala 12. These aircraft did differ from the original four Spanish RF-4Es in that they were fitted with new radios, new RHAW gear, and new VOR/ILS and KS-87 cameras. They also had the smokeless J79-GE-15E engines. The RF-4Cs were steadily repainted in the pale grey livery applied to the nation's Hornet fleet. These improvements allowed the Spanish RF-4C fleet to serve into the 21st century, finally being retired in 2002.

Two Phantoms were kept on QRA (Quick Reaction Alert) duties at all times to defend

F-4EJ Kai (M099) operated by 302nd Hikotai in a spectacular 'retirement' scheme, March 2019. Hyakuri Air Base, Omitama. (Leo Kiewik)

F-4 Phantom (JASDF RF-4E), 23 August 2003, US Yokota Air Base. (Morio)

Right and below right: JASDF F-4EJ(KAI) 37-8315 'Go for It' from 301 Hikotai 'The Frogs' in one of the two special retirement schemes applied to the aircraft. The 301 decommissioning ceremony was conducted on 14 December 2020 at the Hyakuri Air Base in the Iberaki prefecture. (Leo Kiewik)

Republic of Korea Air Force F-4D on display in Dongrak Park in Gumi, South Korea. Note the forward fuselage colour and general camouflage arrangement. (Jakub Skowron)

Spanish air space and were armed with AIM-9J (later AIM-9N) Sidewinder AAMs, AIM-7E Sparrow AAMs and SUU-16A 20mm gun pods.

Turkey

The Turkish Air Force (THK) has operated about 233 F-4s, making it one of the most prolific users of the Phantom II. Under the Peace Diamond I Programme 40 F-4Es were ordered, with deliveries starting in June 1974. Completion of the order was delayed by an arms embargo following the Turkish Invasion of Cyprus. These aircraft equipped 161 *Filo* (squadron) at 6 Ana Jet Us (Jet Aircraft Air Base, also JAB). After that unit upgraded to F-16Cs, these Phantoms moved to 7 JAB for Filo 171 and 172 with Filo 173 providing Operational Conversion Unit (OCU) resources.

Peace Diamond IV was another programme that reinforced the THK and was carried out between June and October 1987. Under the terms of this programme, 40 F-4Es were delivered to Filo 131 and 132, 3 JAB, Konya. Before that, this wing was only a training unit equipped with the last Turkish F-100s; after the conversion it became an operational force.

Turkey also took delivery of a number of former German Air Force RF-4Es.

Early crew training was undertaken by the Simsek Flight (Simsek Kit'a) within 1 JAB at Eskisehir which was disbanded by 1987. The 1977 procurement order saw 32 more F-4E Phantom IIs and 8 RF-4Es acquired under Peace Diamond III, serving mainly with three squadrons of 1 JAB at Eskisehir. These were replacements for F-100D Super Sabres and Northrop RF-5As in 111 and 112 squadrons and the reconnaissance aircraft with 113 Squadron. A milestone was reached when one of the THK Phantom aircraft, 77-0290, became the 5,000th Phantom of the type to be delivered, coinciding with the 20th anniversary, on 27 May 1958, of the first flight of the F-4H.

McDonnell RF-4C Phantom II (Ex 64-1083) of *Ala* (Wing) 12 based at Madrid-Torrejón seen returning from a mission while on deployment to RAF Honington. Last noted in storage at Torrejón. (Mike Freer Touchdown-aviation)

Turkey assisted in Desert Storm without participating in the fighting directly, by opening their air bases to the coalition air forces and hosting Belgian Mirages, German Alpha Jets and Italian F-104Gs. As a reward for their help another 40 former US Air Force Phantoms were delivered to 112 and 172 squadrons, beginning on 25 March 1991. At that time the USAF was phasing out large quantities of older

Above: Turkish Air Force F-4E, 10 July 2008. (Jerry Gunner)

Below: McDonnell Douglas F-4E Phantom II (77-0278) of 1 AHU, THK at Air Fete 1996. (Mike Freer *Touchdown Aviation*)

aircraft, reducing their strength by over 1,000 F-4C/D/Es. These aircraft were desirable to countries like Turkey who already had F-4 fleets, even if they were quite old.

Many of the Turkish Phantoms were used as ground-attack aircraft, a role they performed well due to the systems installed. The first Phantoms delivered to the THK had South East Asia camouflage colours and TISEO equipment, consisting of a wing-mounted television camera with zoom capacity for spotting targets outside normal visual range. The F-4s acquired from US Air Force stocks were former 110th and 141st Tactical Fighter Squadron aircraft (Missouri and New Jersey Air National Guard squadrons respectively) and arrived painted in 'Egyptian One' camouflage, an air-superiority paint scheme consisting of two different shades of blue, despite being best suited for ground attack. The last batch delivered had AVQ-23A Pave Spike laser designation pod compatibility.

On 22 June 2012, the Turkish government announced that Syrian forces had shot down a Turkish RF-4E from 113 Squadron with two crew members over the Mediterranean off the coast of Hatay Province which borders the Syrian Latakia Governorate. The aircraft was reported to have been conducting a reconnaissance flight off the Syrian coast. The Turkish release suggested that the Turkish government did not immediately view the Syrian action as provocative, and it acknowledged that Syrian assets were assisting efforts to find the aircraft and crew. The Syrian Armed Forces made a statement carried by the official Syrian Arab News Agency crediting its anti-aircraft gunners with downing an unidentified aircraft flying at 'very low altitude and at high speed' over Syria's territorial waters toward land less than a mile offshore, causing it to crash into the sea west of the village of Om al-Tuyour. Syrian Foreign Ministry spokesman Jihad Makdissi said 'the downing was an accident, caused by the automatic response of an officer commanding an anti-aircraft gun. The man saw a jet coming at him at high speed and low altitude and opened fire'. The statement went on to claim that the aircraft was found to be a 'Turkish military plane that entered Syrian airspace and was dealt with according to laws observed in such cases'. The downing occurred at a time of heightened tensions between the two countries due to Turkish support for Syrian rebels opposed to the Bashar al-Assad regime in Damascus. On 24 June the wreckage of the F-4 was located in Syrian waters but the crew was not found.

On 24 February 2015 two RF-4Es crashed in the Malatya region in southeast Turkey under unknown circumstances, killing all four crew members. On 5 March 2015 an F-4E-2020 crashed in central Anatolia killing both crew members. Calls to scrap the F-4s and replace them with the fifth generation F-35s were renewed.

Civilian operators

One aircraft, an F-4D (civilian registration N749CF), is operated by the Massachusetts-based non-profit organization Collings Foundation as a living history exhibit. Funds to maintain and operate the aircraft, which is based in Houston, Texas, are raised through donations and sponsorships from public and commercial parties. The financial and technical costs and expertise of maintaining and flying such a complex aircraft must render a future flying programme questionable.

The F-4 legacy

As of 2021, 63 years after its first flight, the F-4 remains in active service with the air forces of Iran, South Korea, Greece and Turkey. The aircraft has most recently been in service against the Islamic State group in the Middle East. There can be few other military aircraft produced that have created such a lasting legacy and the F-4 Phantom II seems set to be with us for a few years to come.

An F-4D owned by the Collings Foundation taxis at Selfridge ANGB, Michigan in May 2005. The plane has the markings of the Steve Ritchie/Chuck DeBellevue fighter from the Vietnam War. (Jacobst)

F-4E Phantom II, Royal Australian Air Force. This fighter-bomber served in the Royal Australian Air Force between 1970 and 1973 with 1 and 6 squadrons, RAAF Base, Amberley, Queensland. In total, 24 Phantoms were leased to the RAAF from the US whilst awaiting the arrival of the F-111C bombers. The aircraft were finished in USAF Phantom II South East Asia colours: FS34102 medium green, FS34079 dark green and 30219 dark tan upper surfaces over FS36622 camouflage grey undersides.

F-4E Phantom II, Egyptian Air Force. The USA offered 35 former USAF F-4Es and the necessary weapons and spares package to the Egyptians. Deliveries began rapidly: the first 18 F-4Es arrived in Egypt in September 1979. All the aircraft were taken from the 31st Tactical Fighter Wing. In the Egyptian Air Force they were assigned to 76 and 78 squadrons, based at Cairo West, through 222 Tactic Fighter Brigade. Originally painted in the South East Asia camouflage scheme, Egyptian F-4Es subsequently received a camouflage pattern known as Egypt-1 which later developed into Hill Gray.

RF-4E Phantom II, German Air Force. The German RF-4E was equipped similarly to the USAF RF-4Cs, using the latest F-4E airframe and more powerful engines. The RF-4Es were employed as day/night reconnaissance aircraft, equipped with four cameras covering 180 degrees. Deliveries were completed in May 1972. The camouflage pattern depicted shows FS36081 dark grey; FS34102 light green and FS34079 dark green.

F-4F Phantom II, German Air Force. In April 1975 deliveries started to Jagdbombergeschwader 36 (Fighter Bomber Wing 36), or JaboG 36 (FBW 36), Rheine-Hopsten and finally JaboG 35, Pferdsfeld. Operationally, the F-4Fs used by JG.71 and JG.74 were employed in the air-to-air role, while those used by JaboG 35 and 36 were used in air-to-air and air-to-ground roles. The camouflage pattern depicted shows: RAL 6005 olivgrun; FS34079 dark green and RAL 7021 schwarzgrun.

RF-4E Phantom II, German Air Force. The German Air Force RF-4E fleet underwent many changes in colour schemes from base greens through to greys and this aircraft is seen in NORM 83A which consists of FS36081 dark grey; FS34102 light green and FS34079 dark green.

F-4E Phantom II, Hellenic Air Force. The Phantom entered service with the Hellenic Air Force in 1974 under the arms programme Peace Icarus. Although it is a second-generation aircraft, 36 Hellenic Phantoms have been upgraded with advanced electronics (Peace Icarus 2000), extending their operational life. They are based at Andrabida Air Base with 117 Combat Wing, 338 and 339 squadrons with call signs Aris and Aias respectively, and at Larissa Air Base with 110 Combat Wing, 337 and 348 squadrons with call signs Ghost and Eyes respectively. After the upgrade programme, all the Hellenic F-4Es wear the Aegean Ghost camouflage pattern while all the Hellenic RF-4Es wear the Vietnam camouflage scheme.

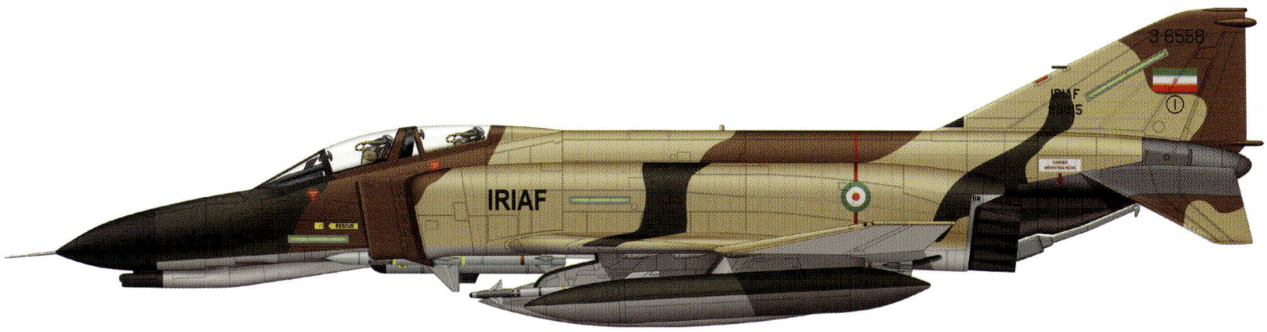

F-4E Phantom II, Islamic Republic of Iran Air Force. In 1970 the first reconnaissance RF-4Es were delivered. Iran, with few fiscal restraints, followed that up with an order for 177 F-4Es. The first of these arrived in March 1971. During a border clash in June 1975, these F-4s, armed with AGM-65 Maverick missiles, defeated an Iraqi armoured ground formation. The F-4Es changed the balance of power in the region; they were effective on the battlefield and were available in large numbers. Aircraft were painted FS30400 sand, FS30140 dark brown and FS34079 dark green on their upper surfaces with FS36622 grey undersides.

Kurnass 2000 (F-4E) Phantom II, Israeli Air Force. Modernized Israeli F-4Es with AN/APG-76 radar and AGM-142 Popeye capability, these entered service in 1989 and were retired in 2004. The camouflage scheme is very appealing; these marketings are available to the modeller from IsraDecal. The camouflage scheme consists of FS30219 brown, FS34227 green and FS33531 tan upper surfaces with FS35622 blue undersides.

F-4EJ Kai Phantom II, Japan Air Self-Defense Force. To upgrade the Phantom fleet the JASDF planned the F-4EJ Kai (meaning modified) programme. This involved 110 aircraft, later reduced to 96, which were upgraded with APG-66 radar, ground attack capabilities and most importantly, ASM-1 or ASM-2 anti-ship missiles (two mounted under the wings). The F-4EJ Kai first flew on 17 July 1984 and entered service on 24 November 1989 with the JASDF 306th Squadron at Komatsu. Some of the most spectacular colour schemes ever applied on military aircraft found their way onto the F-4EJ (Kai). However, this aircraft is the F-4EJ (Kai) in overall greys. More specifically, the camouflage pattern consists of FS36320 grey upper surfaces, a black nose radome and FS36375 grey undersides.

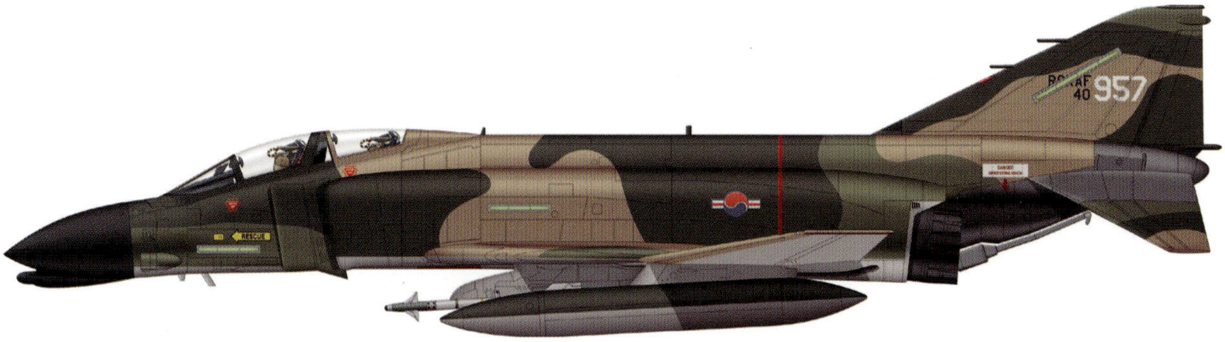

F-4D Phantom II, Republic of Korea Air Force. In the 1960s McDonnell Douglas F-4D Phantom fighter-bombers were introduced and in 1974 they were followed up with the F-4E. Here you can see an F-4D in standard South East Asia camouflage colours: FS34102 medium green, FS34079 dark green upper surfaces with FS36622 grey undersides.

RF-4C Phantom II, Republic of Korea Air Force. The South Koreans also received RF-4Cs. Twelve former USAF 460 Tactical Reconnaissance Group (disbanded in 1990) aircraft were sent to the South Korean 131st Tactical Reconnaissance Squadron, 39 Tactical Reconnaissance Group at Suwon Air Base, along with another 11 sent later. The camouflage pattern shows FS36320 dark ghost grey and FS36375 light ghost grey over FS36422 light grey undersides.

F-4C Phantom II, Spanish Air Force. Through the Mutual Defense Assistance Program (MDAP), Spain acquired 36 former USAF F-4Cs for the Spanish Air Force (Ejército del Aire). These were the only F-4C models ever exported, even as second-hand examples. The F-4Cs were designated C.12 (C stood for Caza and 12 stood for 12th fighter type in service since the creation of the Ejército del Aire). The F-4Cs were assigned to Escuadrones 121 and 122, Ala 12 (Wing). The South East Asia camouflage colours are applied with a FS34102 medium green and FS34079 dark green upper pattern and FS36622 grey undersides.

F-4E Phantom II, Turkish Air Force. Under the Peace Diamond I Program 40 F-4Es were ordered, with deliveries starting in June 1974. Completion of the order was delayed by an arms embargo following the Turkish invasion of Cyprus. These aircraft equipped 161 Filo (squadron) at 6 Ana Jet Us (Jet Aircraft Air Base or JAB). Turkey continues to operate the F-4E to this day. The camouflage colours show FS36118 gunship grey (darker grey) and FS36375 light ghost grey.

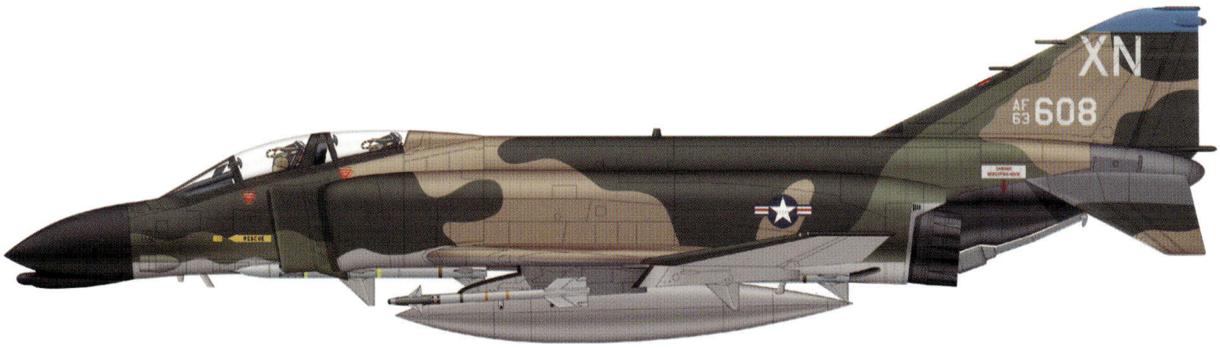

F-4C Phantom II, United States Air Force. The F-4C was essentially identical to the Navy/Marine Corps' F-4B in-flight performance and carried the AIM-9 AAM Sidewinder missile. The first USAF Phantoms in Vietnam were F-4Cs from the 43rd Tactical Fighter Squadron which arrived in December 1964. They carried South East Asia camouflage colours depicted here: FS34102 medium green and FS34079 dark green upper pattern with FS36622 grey undersides. Note the blue fin tip.

F-4D Phantom II, United States Air Force. F-4Ds initially arrived in June 1967 equipped with AIM-4 Falcons, although these AAMs were less than successful. The F-4Ds reverted to using Sidewinders under the Rivet Haste Program in early 1968. By 1972 the AIM-7E-2 Dogfight Sparrow had become the preferred missile for USAF pilots. Like other Vietnam War Phantoms, the F-4Ds were urgently fitted with radar warning receivers to detect the Soviet-built S-75 Dvina SAMs. The South East Asia camouflage pattern is applied: FS34102 medium green and FS34079 dark green upper pattern with FS36622 grey undersides.

F-4G Phantom II, United States Air Force. F-4Gs were deployed to three active wings. One was stationed at George AFB, Victorville, California, as part of the Rapid Deployment Force. One wing was assigned to USAFE (US Air Forces in Europe) at Spangdahlem Air Base, Germany, and the other to PACAF (Pacific Air Forces) at Clark Air Base, Philippines. F-4Gs from all three bases saw combat during Operation Desert Storm in 1991, successfully protecting strike packages from enemy air defences. A total of 134 F-4G models were converted from F-4Es with the first one flying in 1975. Squadron service began in 1978. Here you see a 'Wild Weasel' from Spangdahlem Air Base. The camouflage scheme is FS36320 neutral grey and FS36118 gunship grey (darker grey).

F-4B Phantom II, United States Navy. On 30 December 1960, the VF-121 'Pacemakers' at NAS Miramar became the first Phantom operator with its F4H-1Fs (F-4As). The VF-74 'Be-devilers' at NAS Oceana became the first deployable Phantom squadron when it received its F4H-1s (F-4Bs) on 8 July 1961. By the time of the Tonkin Gulf incident, 13 of 31 deployable navy squadrons were armed with the type. F-4Bs from *Constellation* made the first Phantom combat sortie of the Vietnam War on 5 August 1964, flying bomber escort in Operation Pierce Arrow. This image shows a US Navy F-4B of VF-41 'Black Aces' in colour scheme FS26440 gull grey and FS27875 insignia white.

F-4J Phantom II, United States Navy. The F-4J improved air-to-air and ground-attack capability. Deliveries began in 1966 and ended in 1972 with 522 built. It was equipped with J79-GE-10 engines with 17,844lbf (79.374kN) thrust, the Westinghouse AN/AWG-10 Fire Control System (making the F-4J the first fighter in the world with operational look-down/shoot-down capability), a new integrated missile control system and the AN/AJB-7 bombing system for expanded ground attack capability. This F-4J of VF-143 'Pukin' Dogs' is finished in standard USN colours of the period: FS26440 gull grey and FS27875 insignia white.

F-4N Phantom II, United States Navy. The F-4B was modernized under Project Bee Line and had the same aerodynamic improvements as the F-4J, including smokeless engines. Its first flight was on 4 June 1972 and 228 were converted in total. Here you see an F-4N from VF-14 'Tophatters'. The 1960s and 1970s saw some of the most attractive and flamboyant paint schemes applied to USN Phantoms during their service life.

F-4S Phantom II, United States Navy. The F-4S model resulted from the refurbishment of 265 F-4Js with J79-GE-17 smokeless engines of 17,900lbf (79.379kN), AWG-10B radar with digitized circuitry for improved performance and reliability, Honeywell AN/AVG-8 Visual Target Acquisition Set or VTAS (world's first operational Helmet Sighting System), classified avionics improvements, airframe reinforcement and leading-edge slats for enhanced manoeuvring. The camouflage scheme is FS36440 gull grey overall.

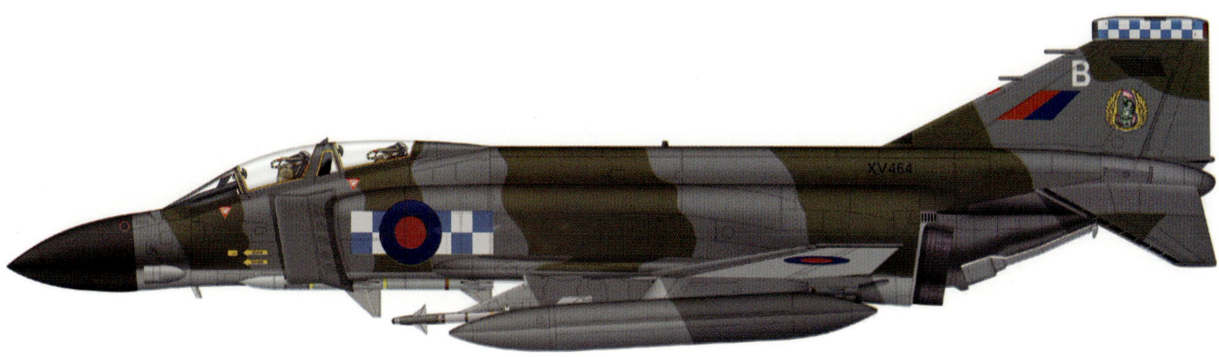

FGR.2 Phantom II, 19(R) Squadron, Royal Air Force circa 1980. The RAF Phantom, given the designation FGR.2, was broadly similar to the naval version (FG.1) with some minor variations in terms of engines, avionics and structure, relevant to its use as a land-based, rather than carrier-based, aircraft. This 19(R) Squadron 'Dolphins' Phantom II was based at RAF Germany and wears the standard BS 381C colour scheme of 241 dark green and BS 381C (638 dark sea grey) over BS 381C (627 light aircraft grey) undersides. The paintwork weathered badly towards the end of their service lives. The blue-chequered pattern in the squadron insignia, although initially dark blue, changed to a sky blue.

FGR.2 Phantom II, 56 Squadron, Royal Air Force. FGR.2s equipped 56 Squadron, the 'Firebirds', and wore the light grey camouflage reflecting its air defence role at that time. The colours shown are BS 381C (241 626 camouflage grey) upper surfaces. Some aircraft additionally had upper, inner wing panels painted BS 381C (637 medium sea grey and BS 381C (627 light aircraft grey).

FG-1 Phantom II, 111 Squadron, Royal Air Force. Former Royal Navy FG.1 aircraft went to 23 'Fighting Cocks' and 111 'Treble One' squadrons in the air defence role. Both initially sported the dark green and dark sea grey upper surfaces over light aircraft grey undersides. This gave way to the light grey scheme: BS 381C (241 626 camouflage grey) upper surfaces. Some, and far from all, aircraft additionally had upper, inner wing panels painted BS 381C (637 medium sea grey) and BS 381C (627 light aircraft grey).

FG.1 Phantom II, 767 Naval Air Squadron, Fleet Air Arm. Two variants were initially built for the UK: the F-4K (FG.1) variant was designed from the outset as an air defence interceptor to be operated by the FAA from the Royal Navy's aircraft carriers. The F-4M (FGR.2) version was procured for the RAF to serve in the tactical strike and reconnaissance role. This 767 NAS, Fleet Air Arm FG.1 Phantom II wears camouflage FS35052 dark sea blue upper surfaces, a black nose radome and FS37875 white undersides.

Modelling the F-4 Phantom II

Introduction

I have been a scale modeller for a long time and I can't think of a time when there weren't models of the F-4. In the early days, Airfix, Monogram and Revell all had reasonable models of the type, depending on your budget.

Certain characteristics, such as raised panel lines, a generally good fit and bright markings that were typical of the US Navy F-4Bs and F-4Js of the time, were the hallmark and set the standard for F-4 modelling. Monogram almost always had decent enough moulded cockpit details and the fit was mostly good. Airfix, on the other hand, had models that looked (and were) pretty accurate in shape and look but suffered from indifferent fit of parts, an excess of raised rivets and a lack of detail in the cockpit.

While these early kits come and go, occasionally being re-released, as Airfix is doing with their current Vintage Classic series, you may be lucky enough to pick up one or more of these early releases if you search the internet: look under tables and in kit swaps at model shows and conventions.

Time moves on though and time has been good for anyone interested in building an accurate, well-detailed model of the F-4 today. Some of the very best quality models are currently available for the F-4 in multiple versions from manufacturers such as Zoukei-Mura, Academy, Tamiya, Finemolds and Revell.

The major scales of 1/72, 1/48 and 1/32 bring you a wide choice of F-4 Phantom II kits in a multitude of markings. Indeed, with the retirement of the F-4 from most air forces around the world – some of course still fly the type such as Turkey, South Korea and Iran – has come a resurgence of new releases and re-boxed re-releases of the Phantom, representing some outstanding retirement schemes. Great examples include the German Air Force F-4F 1/72 kits from Revell through to the sublime Zoukei-Mura F-4EJ Kai Phantom II 'Phantom Forever'.

(David Muscroft)

Left: F-4F Phantom II, 37+16 is from WTD 61 (test and evaluation unit 61). (Thomas Pölkemann)

The Albatros D.V fighter aircraft of Hans von Hippel, Jasta 5. (B. Huber)

F-4F Phantom II, 37+03 50 year FW71 'Richthofen'. (Thomas Pölkemann)

(Leo Kiewik)

One of the biggest attractions is the variety of kits that have been, and continue to become, available in all the major scales. Others must surely be that brutish 'Rhino' look of the type and some of the most spectacular paint schemes and markings that have been applied to a military aircraft – rivalled only by those of the various German Jagdstaffel (Jasta) First World War biplanes that flew in 'Richthofen's Circus'.

The profile of an Albatros D.V clearly shows why JG I became known as The Flying Circus. Having said that, the German Air Force has always had fun applying incredible schemes to their aircraft.

Germany wasn't the only country to get creative with their aircraft commemoration and retirement schemes: Japan runs a close second.

The simple reality of building any scale model is that the manufacturers come and go, as do their kits, and not all kits are available all the time. The good news is that many manufacturers not only re-release their kits at some point or another but they also almost always feature new decals and, on occasion, new parts. Better still, manufacturers like Airfix seem to be going through a careful programme of releasing new-tool kits for subjects that they first released many years ago. Happily these include their British 1/72 F-4 kits: RAF FGR.2 and Royal Navy FG.1.

Additionally, other manufacturers collaborate to release what might appear to be a new kit, although in fact the kit might come from one company and the decals, resin and photo-etch accessories from the other. A great example of this is Eduard from the Czech Republic. They released the very good Academy F-4 along with some very nice aftermarket accessories.

Included are build projects that feature some of the very best kits currently available for the F-4 in 1/72, 1/48 and 1/32 scales.

M099 operated by 302nd Hikotai in a spectacular retirement colour scheme. The unit ceased Phantom operations the following day and reformed at Misawa with the F-35 Lightning.

F-4EJ Kai 07-8436 'Phantom Forever' seen right at the end of its flying career in 2020. A magnificent photo that certainly makes you want to get hold of the Zoukei-Mura 1/48 kit that comes with this scheme. (Kongou Tomoaki)

F-4EJ Kai 37-8315 'Go for It!!' Another JASDF retirement scheme. (Kongou Tomoaki)

Kit: Academy
F-4B Phantom II 153037, VMFA-314 Marines
1/48 scale
Kit Ref: 12232 'VF-111 Sundowners'
Model by Adam Waistell-Brown

Accessories used:

- Eduard Brassin AIM-9B Sidewinder AAMs (648028)
- Eduard Brassin resin wheels
- Quickboost resin seats

The build starts by attaching the side consoles onto the cockpit tub, as the kit is moulded in three different

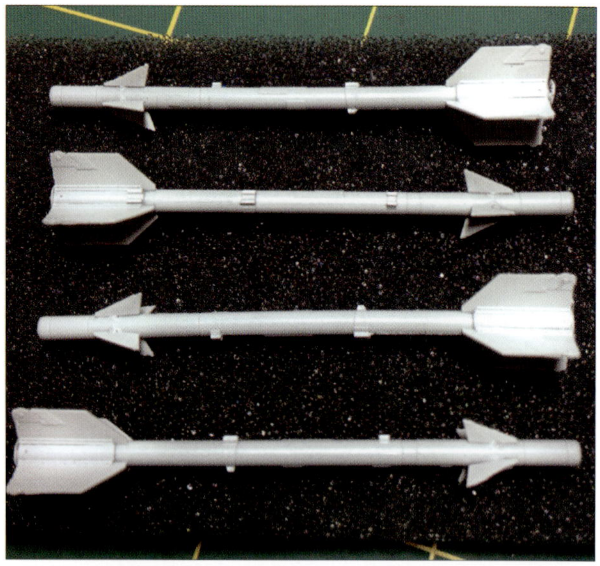

colours (Multi Coloured Plastic); the consoles are in black while the tub is light grey, for modellers who choose not to paint their F-4.

The ejection seats are really quite good and make up an excellent representation of the Martin Baker seat, but as I had a set of spare Quickboost resin seats, these would be added later.

Then comes an interesting discovery: the bottom of the wings and underside of the fuselage is all one mould, except for the front section. This you have to attach to the rear half and line up yourself as there are no locating tabs and actually very little contact at all with the front. Care is needed here to ensure a snug fit (and use a strong glue). This can only mean Academy are going to be kitting a whole range of 1/48 F-4 Phantoms.

The whole fuselage is in one big seamless mould, very much like the Tamiya 1/32 kit, and is really very nice. The only work needed here is to add the in-flight refuelling probe housing; this also needed careful lining up to avoid a nasty step.

The instrument panel detail is not bad but could have that little bit more detail if you choose to have the canopies open; the rest of the cockpit is a little bland to be honest, but a resin update set will rectify this.

The tub can now be added to the lower fuselage half and the intakes, which Academy have tried but failed in attempting to make seamless. Having said that, they are much better than the Hasegawa offering. The rear jet pipes are painted Alclad2 Aluminium and then sprayed with Clear Green, and these are then put into place.

Before you add the top halves of the wings you'll need to make up the main wheel bays; this is no easy feat so be patient and go slow as it's easy to slip up. You'll also need to add the main undercarriage legs at this point as per instructions but they can be added afterwards.

The one-piece top half of the fuselage is now added to the bottom and it fits very well with no filler needed. The intake fairings are added next and require some delicate aligning to eliminate the need to sand the detail away while trying to get a flush finish.

Academy have supplied an array of different radomes and chin blisters, so do your research and check references to make sure your airframe has the right radome and blister combo; this also applies to the fairing on the top of the tail section.

One of the Phantom's most prominent features is the area behind the exhausts, which is unpainted due to heat; there are many methods to recreate this finish.

The main area was sprayed with Alclad2 Steel and some of their heat colours were used. After studying photos of the real thing I used some AK interactive chipping fluid over the steel and sprayed a mix of dark grey and brown over the chipping effects. A small stiff brush was then dampened and stippled to achieve the chipping effect on the exhaust area, looking at the photo all the time to make sure not to overdo the look. The same thing was done with the exhausts, which respond well to the effect.

Hand-mask the canopy using tape and Gunze masking solution and attach the four canopy parts to the cockpit area using PVA glue.

The two-tone grey-white scheme was sprayed on using Gunze acrylics (Light Grey H324 and White H316) and once dry it was all sealed with several coats of Klear ready for the decals, but just before that the anti-glare panel in front of the pilot's screen was sprayed.

The decals were a bit disappointing as there was only one scheme so Furballs 'USMC Rhinos' sheet was used instead. They are beautiful decals to work with. The VMFA-314 markings were chosen: this unit operated from Chu Lai AB in Vietnam in 1968. The hundred or more stencils which are supplied on the Academy sheet were still used; these also performed flawlessly. It took me a night to add them all but it doesn't look right without them. The whole model then got another coat of Klear to protect the decals and was left to dry overnight before the weathering process began.

MiG Productions' dark wash was added to all panel lines in a capillary action as painting adds too much wash to the area and can look overdone. After an hour the wash was tidied up with a cotton bud and a coat of matt varnish was misted on.

The kit wheels are a little disappointing. Fortunately Eduard had just released a new Brassin wheel set for the Academy Phantom. They really do look so much better than the kit efforts and come with wheel chocks if you wish to display them on a base. Some careful painting brings out the crisp detail Eduard have created in this lovely add-on.

Also bought were four Brassin AIM-9 Sidewinders to replace the kit missiles, although the missiles supplied with the kit are fine. The Eduard Brassin missiles come with resin seeker covers and photo-etch 'Remove before Flight' tags.

This model sports four AIM-9s and three fuel tanks for the load out; bombs were going to be added but the kit offering wasn't convincing. Brassin Mk.82s have since been released.

Finally a little wear and tear, in the form of a tiny brush and some Vallejo dark grey in the areas that would take a battering, was added. Academy has stolen the quarter-scale crown from Hasegawa's long-established F-4 series. Of course, Tamiya is about to release an all-new tool F-4B in mid-2021 and that's sure to be an excellent kit, especially if you find this Academy release difficult to get hold of.

00
VW
3037
VMFA-314
COL NORM GOURLEY
MARINES
00

00
VW
VMFA-314
COL NORM GOURLEY
3037
00
MARINES
153037

00
VW
VMFA-314
COL NORM GOURLEY
3037
MARINES
153037

00
VW
3037
COL NORM GOURLEY
MARINES
153037

00
VW
3037
VMFA-314
MARINES
00

Kit: Tamiya
F-4B Phantom II, US Navy
1/48 scale
Kit Ref: 61121
Model by George Canare

The model kit is a true work of art from the engineering of details to the accuracy of shape and the finesse of parts fitment. The breakdown of the seams is well mannered, leaving little to address and not much loss of surrounding details. The fuselage breakdown speculates for planned future variations. The cockpit execution is precise and exacting, staying true to the to the F-4B Phantom II of the 1972 airframe. The colour mix ratios called out in the kit are similar colours found throughout the Tamiya range of 1/48 aircraft kits of recent release.

Addressing the sprue attachment points is critical to safeguard precise fitment; the multiple dry-fitting of parts will help minimize the clean-up of seams. Don't rush: take the time to enjoy the thoughtfulness of the model designers to ensure a rewarding experience.

The exhaust nozzles require close attention in removing the sprue attachment point as over-sanding will result in an unnecessary gap. Take care to remove the nubs from the air intake as pointed out in the instructions. The horizontal stabilizer and ancillary parts can be assembled and finished separately with final attachment as a part of the conclusion of the build. Other parts that can be finished separately and added to the assembly are the vertical stabilizer, landing gear, drop tank, weapon pylons and rails.

In step 46 close attention to the AIM-7E Sparrow fitment needs to be observed for correct placement. In this model the separation stripe from the kit decals for the ejection seat pull ring handles has been used and a snug fit achieved with Mark Fix Strong. The finished model kit was completed with all Tamiya products from paint, cement, liquid surface primer and decal solutions. The kit decals work well and the additional layer of TS-13 or LP-9 Clear will protect and help with the use of Panel Line Accent colours.

NL
0456
USS CORAL SEA
VF-51
NAVY
COMMANDER ATTACK CARRIER
AIR WING FIFTEEN
001
100

STRAW
DOGS
00
NL
0456
USS CORAL SEA
VF-51
NAVY
001

00
NL
0456
USS CORAL SEA
VF-51
NAVY
COMMANDER ATTACK CARRIER
AIR WING FIFTEEN
100

Kit: Academy
F-4C converted to EF-4C
1/48 scale
Kit Ref: 12294
Model by Sung Ho Park

Accessories used:

- GT resin F-4C Wild Weasel conversion parts
- Monokio F-4C Wild Weasel decal
- Eduard AGM-45 kit

F-4Cs were converted into Wild Weasel ECM aircraft. They were equipped with AN/APR-25 RHAWS, an AN/APR-26 missile launch warning system, an ER-142 ECM receiver and an AN/ALQ-119 external ECM pod. They were armed with AGM-45 Shrike anti-radiation missiles and cluster bombs but were unable to carry the AGM-78 Standard ARM missile. A total of 36 were converted.

The Academy F-4 range of kits were all-new tool productions that started to come out in 2012; this F-4C base kit was released by Academy the following year in 2013. The kit's proportions and detail were satisfactory but not perfect, with re-engraving needed on almost all the fuselage panels. The model does look the part but something a little different was required for this project as the subject of the model was to be the F-4C Wild Weasel. This was achieved by using GT resin parts. You just need to follow the instructions and look at your references to make the conversion look authentic. An ALQ-87 ECM pod is included in the GT resin kit; two AGM-45s from Eduard and two AIM-7 AAMs from the Academy kit were used.

The purpose of the project was to test Tru Color paint; the paint numbers used were as follows: 1209 (FS34102), 1211 (FS36623), 1212 (FS30219), 1213 (FS34079) and Tamiya Gloss Black (X-1) for the nose radome. The paint performs really well, and the colour is much better than anything else that is commonly used in Korea. It was almost the exact colour that was wanted. In terms of weathering, light weathering with oil colour paint and water colour pencil was applied.

The kit is very impressive and this conversion is quite straightforward.

SUPER
COCKS
SWISS
SAMLAR
ZG
AF
40
840

ZG
AF
40
840

ZG
AF
40 840
SUPER
COCKS
SWISS
SAMLAR

SUPER
COCKS
SWISS
SAMLAR

RESCUE
840

SUPER

SUPER
COCKS
SWISS
SAMLAR
840

Kit: Zoukei-Mura
F-4D Phantom II
1/48 scale
Kit Ref: 48-07
Model by Adam Waistell-Brown

This Zoukei-Mura kit is very impressive. The cockpit is the starting point; to get to it the instructions have you making up the front undercarriage bay, which is also the cockpit floor. The level of detail in this cockpit is good; the side console details are some of the best in injection-moulded kits.

The ease of constructing the cockpit assembly really is sublime and in no time one is ready to put some paint on it. An initial coat of Tamiya Nato black then followed by H325 by Gunze was applied. The kit decals for the instruments are used.

The intakes are next; these consist of a top and bottom half and simply join together. Some filler has been used in an attempt to sand them flush, creating a seamless intake. The engines are complete and can be seen through the auxiliary air intake panels on the bottom of the fuselage. First the interior and exterior of the engines were sprayed in Alclad2 Aluminium. The interior was also sprayed with Tamiya Clear Green. After weathering with a little Mig AMMO black pigment, including the afterburner rings, both engines were assembled ready to be fitted onto the bottom fuselage-wing part. Both the intakes and the engines were then fitted to the bottom fuselage section and fixed with Tamiya Extra Thin Quick Setting glue.

The undercarriage bays need to be made up separately. They are perfect. The Academy kit has over-engineered bays with multiple components; these have two parts and have been cleverly moulded. They fit snugly onto the wing assembly and allow for the fitment of the top wing half. (Don't forget to open those pylon holes.)

The F-4 intakes in the scale modelling world are normally a little tricky to fit without having to use filler and sand most of the detail away, leaving the modeller to re-scribe. The Zoukei-Mura kit is not perfect and takes some minor filling but this didn't have to be sanded much at all.

Zoukei-Mura provide the modeller with a choice of dropped flaps and slats which is rather splendid as it can make for an interesting model if everything is hanging down.

Make sure the airframe is free from any blemishes and then add some pre-shading to the underside of the aircraft, just to make the H311 Grey seem a little more interesting. This is lightly sprayed so the pre-shading shows through slightly. This was left to dry for a day or two. Then mask all the grey and start on the South East Asia scheme.

Here H303 Green, H309 Dark Green and H310 Brown have been used for the camouflage which is drawn on freehand. After a few days varnish the entire airframe in Tamiya X-22 Clear mixed with Gunze Self Levelling Thinners.

Allow a week for the varnish to dry properly then start on the metallic area which is very prominent on the F-4 family. Alclad2 Chrome was used after the gloss black base coat was dry.

Xtradecal sheet X48063 includes two aircraft from Lakenheath. One has the South East Asia markings, however the tan was replaced by a light green/brown colour.

One by one the decals were added, and they performed reasonably well although they had trouble settling down, even with some Daco setting solution. The red warning band around the fuselage had some silvering. The arduous task of the countless stencils then began, but the time and effort were worthwhile.

All the decals were sealed in with a coat of clear gloss and left to dry for a couple of days. While that was drying the radome was painted gloss black and after drying the ten decals were added and sealed. The tail fin tip was painted red as per the instructions on the decal sheet.

A panel wash was applied next with a dark wash by Mig AMMO selected. This was applied by using a capillary action and cleaned up using a cotton bud, moistened with a little white spirit where needed. The metallic areas also received a wash using a blue/black from the Mig AMMO metallic aircraft set.

The last few pieces of the Phantom can now be added. The undercarriage units were all painted black followed by a coat of gloss white and the oleo strut was painted with the fabulous Molotow silver pen. The wheels were also masked and painted which could have been upgraded to resin items but the kit wheels looked fairly decent.

The gear doors were fitted after the undercarriage had properly set; it was glued into position as were the arresting hook and the exhaust nozzles, which were both painted in Humbrol Steel Metalcote paint.

The fuel tanks, AIM-9 and AIM-7 missiles were all painted and decaled prior to being added to the finished build; these all look really good and are a credit to Zoukei-Mura. The canopy was then added.

The kit includes some very cleverly engineered parts but it is not clear why Zoukei-Mura include full engines. Overall a fabulous kit and one that looks great straight out of the box.

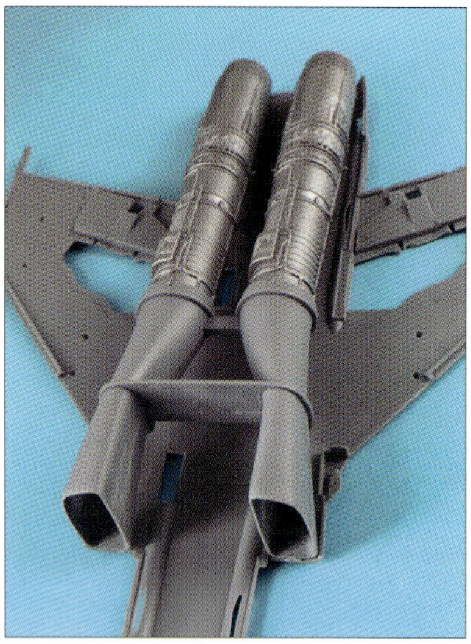

LN
AF
66502

LN
AF
66502

LN
AF
66 502

LN
AF
66 502

RESCUE
0615

Kit: Tamiya
F-4E Phantom II, Hellenic Air Force
1/32 scale
Kit Ref: 60310
Model by Chris Evans

The Greek Phantom underwent a major Avionics Upgrade Programme (AUP) in 1997–2000 to completely upgrade the avionics system. For modellers the biggest impact of this is a brand-new cockpit with new layouts and multi-function displays (MFDs) in both the front and rear cockpits. Bringing this model into the 21st century by converting it to a Greek Hellenic Air Force AUP version required quite a lot of aftermarket parts:

- Eduard Big Ed photo-etch set
- Eduard Brassin exhausts
- Eduard Brassin seats
- Eduard Brassin litening pod
- Eduard Brassin wheels
- GT Resin seamless intakes
- GT Resin slat wing conversion
- Master Pitot probe
- Quickboost mirrors
- QMT Auxiliary intake detail

The fuselage is moulded in one large section, which is very nice. The only anomaly here is the addition of quite a few raised panels. At first glance these look like repair panels, but they aren't. The panels are actually correct but, for some reason, Tamiya have done them as raised when they shouldn't be. Mark all of these panels and sand them off and re-scribe them flush.

The GT Resin seamless intakes require a bit of butchering of the kit fuselage. Use a razor saw on the fuselage to remove the moulded-on intakes. The initial dry-fit of the GT Resin intakes isn't too bad although filling and sanding is required to blend them in. Install the intakes using Araldite epoxy adhesive and once fully cured, blend them in using P38 car body filler: it cures in minutes and is easy to sand.

Then re-scribe all the panels, panel lines and rivets. Here RB Productions Scribe-R with DYMO Tape was used but care had to be taken when scribing over the filler as it had the tendency to break up at the edges. Give it a coat of black primer to check the scribing.

The exhausts were from Eduard Brassin; the single-piece exhaust tubes were a little tricky to paint inside but once dry they were installed into the fuselage in the same manner as the kit parts. The nozzles were left off to install at the end. The Eduard seats have superb detail and include photo-etch seatbelts.

Next came the rear fuselage, particularly the underside exhaust area. Detail was added using parts from the Big Ed set along with some scratch detail using strips of thin aluminium.

To position the drag chute in the open position box it in and add the photo-etch bulkhead.

The rear fuselage was painted at this point. Various shades of Alclad2 were used along with weathering pencils from AK Interactive to achieve different tonal effects and metallic contrasts.

The upgraded AUP cockpit is the most complicated part of this build. With Airscale modern jet cockpit photo-etch parts from the spares box, the instrumentation was produced. New instrument panels, front and rear, were scratch-built and the Big Ed upgrade parts were used for side console detail. Trial fitting is the key here, adjusting the fit until everything lines up and looks good. The multifunction displays were next, scratch-built from plastic card and detailed with Airscale photo-etch parts. A lot of wiring was added using thin solder.

Next, the nose cone. This is moulded in clear plastic to allow you to see the radar and cannon if you wish. Some may find this a bit gimmicky. The Greek version has IFF antennae on the upper surface of the nose and an additional antenna on the cannon fairing underneath. These are scratch-built from plastic card and fixed on centrally. Another fairly big job was to re-model the anti-glare panel and HUD in the front cockpit. The kit part was modified to include an all-new HUD unit, scratch-built and a bit fiddly. A MFD for the front cockpit instrument panel was also built. The seats were temporarily slotted in to check the fit and overall look.

The paint process was kicked off with a primer coat of Mr Surfacer 1500 Black, thinned with levelling thinners. This gives a perfect satin base, and once it was left to cure for a few days, the whole airframe was degreased with Mr Paint MRP Surface Cleaner MRP-DG. At this stage a rough marbling effect was done over the entire surface using MRP light grey colour.

MRP paints were extensively used on this build. They give a perfectly smooth satin finish that is great for applying decals onto. The three-colour Aegean camouflage scheme was hand-sprayed (quite easy on a model of this size) using an Iwata HP-CH brush with 0.2mm nozzle. The three colours are MRP-094 Medium MOD Grey, MRP-105 Grey Blue and MRP-245 Light Sea Grey. The nose cone was done with MRP-097 Dark

Ghost Grey. A great addition that came with the Big Ed photo-etch set were stencils for some of the smaller 'no step' markings.

The details are hand-painted, like the formation lights and antennae. Once the paint had cured for a few days it was again degreased. The decals were from Procal Decals. This is a Greek company that specializes in decals for several Hellenic Air Force aircraft like the F-4, F-16 and Mirage. They are well worth checking out, especially the anniversary schemes. This model's scheme was displayed at the Royal International Air Tattoo in 2017. A nice colourful fin and good-looking drop tanks. From reference photos these Greek F-4s look pretty filthy. The weathering is held back though and kept generally light, just accentuating the panel lines and giving tonal differences to break up the large surface areas and give it a bit of depth. The panel line washes are from AK and Mig in a greyish colour, not too dark before moving onto adding dirt and grime using pastels and powders.

The final additions were the drop tanks, with the Procal Decals, and the canopies and pitot tube from Master. Also added is the centreline drop tank from a Revell kit in my stash as Tamiya does not include this.

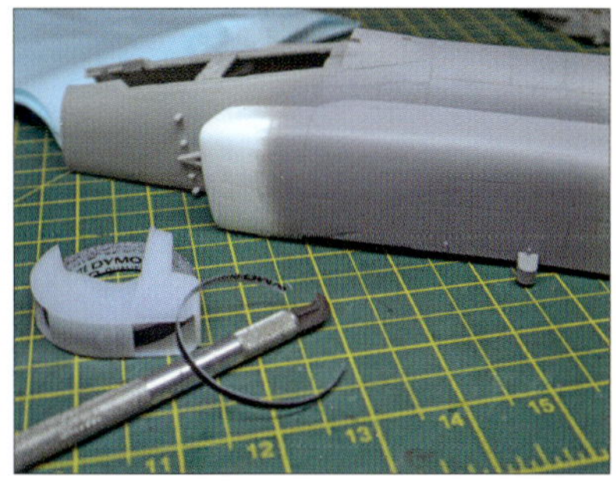

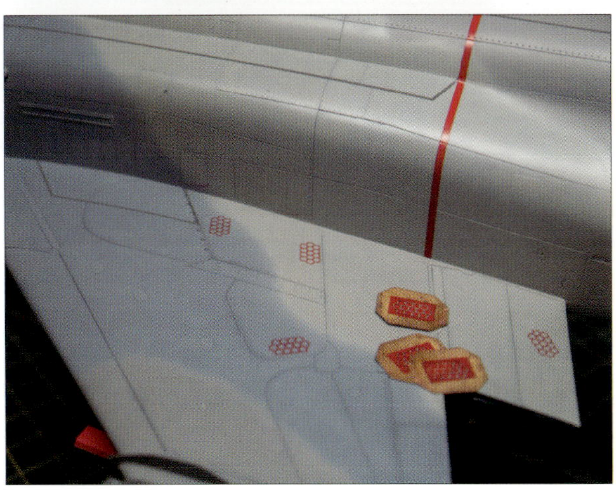

ΠΑ
RESCUE

DANGER
ARRESTING HOOK

ΠΑ
ARES

01508
ΠΑ
AIR TATTOO
ARES

01508
ΠΑ
ΑΡΗΣ
AIR TATTOO
2017

01508
ARES

338
01508

01508
ARES

01508
ΠΑ

01508

ΠΑ

ΠΑ
ARES
AIR TATTOO
2017

Kit: Zoukei-Mura
F-4E Phantom II, early USAF
1/48 scale
Kit Ref: Super Wings Series No.10
Model by Geoff Coughlin

This kit is quite superb and looks every inch an F-4E. The detail is very good and the fit is near perfection – not quite, but close. The kit builds very well out of the box and you really don't need to add much. The main additions are some scratch-building behind the seats where all the wiring looms are located and some belts for the ejection seats. It's useful that Zoukei-Mura provide seats without belts as this enables you to add your own and this model uses some pre-painted items from Eduard. One of the main features in the Zoukei-Mura F-4 kit is the provision of a separate upper fuselage section that drops in and avoids the need for sanding and cleaning up an upper fuselage join that would ruin the beautifully recessed detail.

The provision of exhaust cans with open or closed afterburner plates is a welcome addition. The standard operating procedure for the F-4 is that the exhaust cans are left open when parked; this was only realized after completing the model. The speed brakes are shown in the deployed position as well as the flaps to add a bit of interest.

Most of the weathering on this model makes use of pastel chalk applied with a fine brush which helps create an authentic, subtle weathered look. It's all a matter of personal taste though and some of these F-4Es got pretty manky in South East Asia.

Colonel Steve Ladd, who flew the F-4E in Vietnam, said this model captured the soul of the F-4 perfectly.

Adding canopy locks, available from Eduard as an aftermarket set, would have increased the authenticity of the finished model. These could be scratch-built but Eduard provides a nice photo-etch set that looks good and will save time. The manufacturer's 'Remove before Flight' (RBF) tags have been added and hung from the early Sidewinder missiles in the cockpit and from the undercarriage locks as this is common practice on the real thing. The pilot boarding ladder that's provided in the kit helps finish off the model nicely.

RESCUE
308

RESCUE

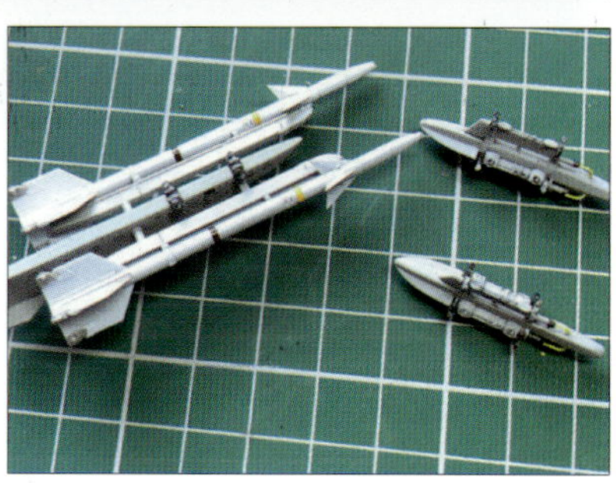

308

JV
AF
70
308

JV
AF 70
308
308

RESCUE

SWS
F-4E Early
PHANTOM II
1/48
SUPER WING SERIES 1/48 No.10

L.T. JACK FISHER
Betty Lou

L.T. JACK FISHER
Betty Lou
CAUTION
NO PUSH

Kit: Zoukei-Mura
F-4EJ Kai Phantom II Phantom Forever 2020
1/48 scale
Kit Ref: Super Wing Series No.11
Model by Geoff Coughlin

Additional parts:

- Eduard photo-etch canopy, seat set (49231)
- Eduard RBF tags (1/72 better scale look)
- Scratch-built details in cockpit and on undercarriage units

Assembling the cockpit is very straightforward; just be sure to take your time securing the parts exactly, so that they line up perfectly and all will be well. The raised detail on all the panels is superb and also works perfectly with the decals provided.

Prepare the cockpit parts by spraying black first and then Dark Sea Grey, allowing some of the shadows to give a decent 3D look. You can add some dry-brushing and then the fine detail painting using a cocktail stick for the various knobs and switches.

The decals settle down really well by first wetting each main panel with Johnson's Klear (or use Micro Set/Sol) and when in position apply heat from a hairdryer. Sounds risky but it isn't really, just a medium heat and not too close. Keep the heat on until the decal draws down fully over the raised detail. It's incredible how this works, even over very pronounced detail.

It's a good idea to add the engine intakes at this point; it's easier to get everything lined up now before you tape it securely. The fit is perfect; you just need to get the join precisely lined up. Unless you plan to do some serious surgery to the airframe, the engines won't be seen. This project is all about the paint scheme so the engines can just be made up and inserted into the airframe without any need for paint. If FOD guards are added to the intake faces there is no need to worry about the insides of the intakes either. The lower wing section, with the engines, attaches to the separate upper wing sections and must be taped up to dry. Again, flawless: no filler at all for the main wing join.

Prepare all the smaller parts like the undercarriage doors, inner faces and the wheel wells and spray them dark grey. Some gloss white will be added later on, and the dark grey will add depth to the final look.

Eduard does a good PE set with plenty of canopy detail. The parts with the hooks just need to be trimmed to fit. Use MRP paints as their black gives a nice contrast to the dark grey used in and around the cockpit area. You have some serious masking to do first to protect the rest of the grey airframe.

It's a good idea to get the base metallic onto the rear underside now: use AK's Xtreme Metal Dark Aluminium for that. Several areas on the underside and the stabilizers will need detail colouring later. Galleria Acrylic Gloss varnish was used before adding the decals. The blue on the wing and centreline tanks needs to be mixed and sprayed to match the decals (Tamiya Clear Blue X-23; Vallejo acrylic White Aluminium).

The kit decal sheet really is something special and the painting/decal guide included in the kit is incredibly helpful. The decals are batched on the sheet which is especially useful when applying all the tiny stencils so you don't have to do much hunting early on. Later, when you've cut the sheet up into small pieces it's useful to try and keep some sort of order on your bench or you'll go mad trying to find some of the smaller items.

The Martin Baker Mk.7 seats provided are a good base on which to build. They need a harness and again, although the overhead ejection handles are provided in plastic, it is impossible to remove and clean these up without damaging them. Eduard comes to the rescue with a nice pre-painted detail set (FE1013).

Now add the prominent wiring behind the pilot and RIO. Drill out some holes in the back of the RIO's instruments to help locate the wires and use fine lead detailing wire for the task.

Other additions include finely coiled wire to represent the oxygen hoses and an Eduard canopy detailing set (a tip is to insert a piece of flexible wire into the coil to help it maintain its shape). This is great because you get the canopy rails, hooks and mirrors that help finish this area nicely. Here a couple of RBF tags have been added for a bit more interest.

The F-4EJ Kai Phantom II in 1/48 scale from Zoukei-Mura is nearly flawless in terms of fit. It has great detail and is a joy to build. Obviously this scheme is something very special and the decals are outstanding quality. You do need to find a seat harness and canopy details as well as adding some extra wiring behind the seats.

(Kongou Tomoaki)

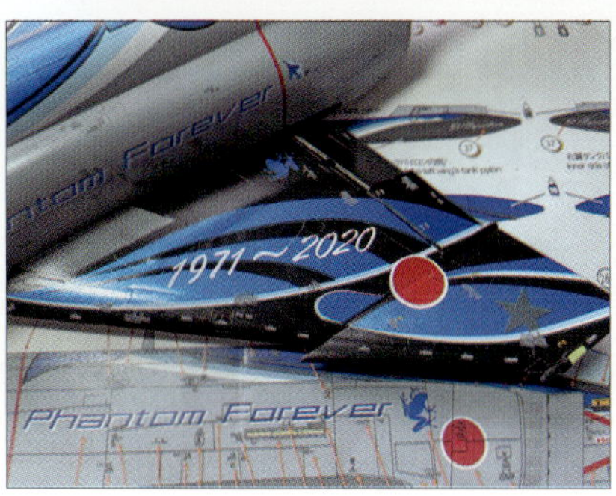

436
Phantom Forever
07-8436

om Forever
JET
DANGER
INTAKE
436

Phantom Forever
Thank you PhantomII

07-8436
1971～2020
Phantom Forever
Thank you Phantom II
436

Thank you Phantom II
Phantom F
436
DANGER

07-8436
436
Phantom Forever

JET
DANGER
INTAKE
436

436

07-8436
Phantom Forever

Phantom Forever

07-8436

07-8436
301Squadron

07-8436
Phantom Forever
436

436
JET
DANGER
RESCUE
INTAKE
ARMAMENT

Thank you Phantom II
436
Phantom Forever
1971 ~ 2020

Thank you Phantom II
436

Phantom Forever
you Phantom II

Phantom Fore
Thank you Phantom II

07-8436
2020

JET
DANGER
INTAKE
436

07-8436

Kit/ Hasegawa
F-4G 'Wild Weasel' USAF
1/72 scale
Kit ref/ 04108
Model by Adam Waistell-Brown

The 1/72 Hasegawa kit is still pretty good and holds up well. It comes with a basic cockpit with very little detail and so resin ejection seats by Quickboost have been added, instead of the kit seats that are basic, even for the small scale. When it comes to the main instrument panels, decals are included that will look perfectly acceptable in this scale, even with the canopy open; you have the option for open or closed canopies from the box contents.

As you'd expect, the cockpit tub is fitted between the forward fuselage halves and it's always worth adding some nose weight to stop your F-4 model tail-sitting. The big G-model nose cone makes this very easy; get the centre of gravity well forward so less weight is needed to achieve the task.

There are a host of aftermarket accessories for the F-4 in 1/72 scale so choose ones that make the biggest impact to the look of the finished model. This build includes some very nice resin afterburner (reheat) cans as they have excellent detail. The intakes are almost always separate items in F-4 kits and they fitted quite well on this G-model – just remember to paint the insides white if you aren't going to add FOD (Foreign Object Damage) guards to the engine intakes.

Metallic areas were sprayed using AK Extreme Steel and masking tape strips were added to the exhaust area then sprayed in a darker shade of steel to help create the varied metallic and burnt metal tones of the real aircraft. The exhausts themselves are finished using the AK Steel with a light overspray of grey to give that used look. The main painting is pretty straightforward; here Gunze paints H306 is used followed by H305 grey and when all was totally dry the model was given a good coat of Tamiya X-22 Clear gloss varnish ahead of the decal application. Be sure to leave the gloss to dry completely, then apply the many decals. More gloss varnish must be used to seal in the decals when they are dry, followed by a coat of flat varnish to tone everything down.

To finish up, various panels are picked out using Mig's AMMO panel line wash and when your weathering is complete, the undercarriage can be fitted along with doors and any stores you may want to add. On this model a centreline and wing tanks, plus the air-to-air missiles (AAMs), have been added. The last job is to attach the canopies, making sure they are aligned correctly if displayed open – this is a common mistake on F-4 kits.

SP
AF
295

Kit: Tamiya
F-4J Phantom II
1/32 scale
Kit Ref: 60308 (or 60306)
Model by Dariusz Kowalczuk

This model is built straight from the box. The kit itself dates back to 1997 and was released to huge acclaim by modellers because it was the first time we had a good quality kit of the famous F-4J Phantom II in 1/32 scale.

Perhaps the most startling thing about the Tamiya F-4 kit in this scale is the creative way the manufacturer tackled the fuselage, being moulded in one piece, completely unheard of before. This model also features recessed panel lines. The kit became available again three years later in 2000 with new US Marines markings and stores. There are a few simple corrections to make, like removing the raised moulded panels on the fuselage side, but overall this is a very good kit. The general belief is that Tamiya engineers might have taken as their reference an F-4J airframe that had battle damage repair patches that led them to mould these onto the kit fuselage sides believing them to be standard on the airframe. Whatever the reason, it's a simple matter to sand back these panels and re-scribe any lost details.

As mentioned, this model was built pretty much straight from the box, although you can always add details and there are many aftermarket sets available from several manufacturers like Eduard and Aires. The areas that would benefit most from an upgrade, should you wish to go there, are resin seats and perhaps a full cockpit. Apart from that the afterburner (reheat) cans at the back could look a little more refined with resin aftermarket items.

You'll notice that the model is pretty weathered and how far one goes is, as always, a matter of personal taste. Operational F-4s, especially those operated from aircraft carriers at sea, weathered pretty heavily and this creates a great opportunity for modellers to capture an authentic look. Paints like Hataka Hobby wash and other products for weathering from Tamiya and Gunze completed the weathered effects on show.

16
NF
5579
USS MIDWAY
155579
VF-151
NAVY
DANGER
INTAKE
216

16
NF
5579
155579
VF-151
NAVY

216
DANGER
INTAKE

NF
16

Kit: Zoukei-Mura
F-4J Phantom II US Marines
1/48 scale
Kit Ref: (SWS48 No.08)
Model by Dave Coward
(additional photos Manuel Magrinho)

Marine Fighter Attack Squadron 232 (VMFA-232) is a United States Marine Corps Squadron nicknamed the 'Red Devils'; it is the oldest and most decorated fighter squadron in the Marine Corps. Aftermarket products used for this model include:

- Eduard F-4 Steel seatbelts ED49111
- Master pitot tubes MR48049
- Eduard Brassin F-4J weighted wheels ED648313
- Neware exhaust nozzle masks MWAM 0333
- Modeltools ejection seat wire
- Eduard Steel 'RBF' tags (1/72 scale)

The kit ejector seats are missing any form of seatbelts, either in the form of moulded detail or photo-etch. A set of Eduard's pre-painted steel belts was used. In addition, the oversized ejection seat handles were removed with twisted wire and some 'Remove before Flight' tags from Eduard were added to give a busier look to the seats.

The kit has two options from the box for the side consoles and instrument panels: decals or raised detail that's very nicely done. A combination has been used on this model to get the best result; the decals for the pilot's instrument panel were cut into small segments and overlaid on the raised detail. Daco's strong decal solution was used to get them to settle into the surface detail. When dry, extra detail was added with carefully applied paint. Gloss paint is used over the dials to get a glass effect. For the side consoles the decals were quite plain so these were painted with acrylics. The pilot's and WSO's radar displays were first painted in silver, then Tamiya clear orange and finally covered with clear epoxy to get a nice domed glass effect.

Zoukei-Mura's use of an insert for the fuselage spine is a lovely addition; it replicates the panel lining on the real aircraft and stops any issues that come with the loss of detail a traditional join along the centre produces when you sand the area flush.

The painting process was pretty straightforward. Prime the airframe, tail surfaces, wing pylons, fuel tanks and gear doors with Tamiya Fine White Primer. Spray the underside and all other areas that need to be white with Mr Paints White. Mask off the airframe underside using the Blu-Tac method to get a slightly feathered demarcation between the upper and lower camouflage colours. The areas that needed to be red were also masked off with tape to get a hard demarcation line. Note that the kit has decals for the red areas at the wing and elevator tips, the intake lips and the canopy sides but these areas were sprayed on this model so as to keep the red consistent with the tail colour. Then spray the upper grey (FS16440) again using Mr Paints colours. The elevator upper surfaces were also sprayed grey. Mask off the areas that need to be red (tail, intake lips, wing and elevator tips) and spray them with Mr Paints US Navy Red. Remove the masking tape and do any touch-ups that are required. The bare metal tail area and the inner area of the elevators were sprayed with various metal shades from Alclad2 and then tinted with their Hot Metal colours.

The extendable ladder that was an option in the kit was not used, as reference photos of these aircraft showed they used the larger detachable types on shore-based aircraft. The kit has these on a sprue as unused parts so they were used, along with some helmets from True Details that were sprayed white.

13

WT
VMFA-232
3833
13
MARINES

Zoukei-Mura have released other boxings of this F-4J kit, including this one nicely finished by Manuel Magrinho

(Aurelio Reale)

Kit/ Tamiya
F-4J Phantom II converted to RAF 74 Squadron F-4J(UK)
1/32 scale
Kit Ref: Tamiya 60308 (2000)
Model by Dave Coward

Aftermarket products used:

- Aires F-4J cockpit
- Aires F-4J exhausts
- Yellow Hammer RAF F-4J Phantoms
- Eduard Brassin F-4 resin wheels
- Aero Bonus Sidewinder covers
- Quickboost intake covers
- Two Bobs Aim-9 and AIM-7 decals

You can't beat a resin replacement for the cockpit in this scale as there is just so much visible, especially with an open canopy. Adding the Aires resin cockpit will require a lot of sanding and adjustment to get a decent fit.

If there is one weakness with this kit it is the intakes. A lot of work is required if you want to eliminate the seams in the interior trunking. Aftermarket seamless intakes are available or, if you want to model the aircraft on the ground, use intake blanks to cover up the offending holes. A set from Quickboost which are the same will work well and reflect those in reference photos.

The Yellow Hammer 74 Squadron decals were a little brittle and real care had to be taken in order to prevent them from breaking up when positioning them. They also didn't respond that well to softeners such as Micro Sol so several coats of Daco Products Strong Decal Setting Solution had to be used. Another issue is the decals only cover the main markings and have no stencilling or warning markings, so it was time to raid the spares box. The end result is that the decals aren't 100 per cent accurate but they look better than none at all.

One very obvious addition to later-model RAF Phantoms is the periscope for the navigator. This is located on the left-hand side of the central canopy support structure. Basically the left window has been removed and an insert fitted where the periscope has been situated. There was no aftermarket replacement available so it had to be scratch-built.

The kit contains all the air-to-air weapons you would expect to see on a Phantom but there is one problem: the kit has AIM-9B Sidewinders and UK Phantoms used AIM-9Ls. Luckily aftermarket replacements are readily available.

When on the ground, oleo locks were fitted to both main gear retraction arms and the nose gear retraction arm. Again, it was back to scratch-building. These were made from brass tubing (Albion Alloys) and Evergreen plastic strip. The retraction arms were cut in two and the ends were fitted into the fabricated locks. To finish them more 'Remove before Flight' tags were added along with some spare decals. The main legs are from the kit and are made from metal: good job given the weight of this kit. The kit wheels are rubber and are not bad but they were replaced with resin ones from Eduard Brassin which are much more detailed.

REMOVE BEFORE FLIGHT
R

RESCUE
R

R
ZE354

Kit: Hasegawa
F-4S Phantom II
1/48 scale
Kit Ref: Hasegawa 07355 (2014)
Model by David W. Aungst

Aftermarket products used:

- KMC resin cockpit
- KMC weapons pylons
- AiRes resin exhausts
- Assorted decals (Airframe Data Markings)

The camouflage pattern for a UH-1N in the USMC black-green-grey is the same basic pattern used in the USAF European green-grey scheme. Which aircraft share both of these camouflage patterns? The list is very short: UH-1, CH-53 and OV-10 or all the aircraft that were shared between the USAF and USMC. Each of these aircraft has similar basic pattern in which the colours are simply translated. The colour translations as follows:

USAF – USMC
D. Green (F.S.34079) – Marine Green (F.S.34097)
M. Green (F.S.34102) – Black (F.S.37038)
D. Grey (F.S.36081) – D. Ghost Grey (F.S.36320)

The USAF had a standard European green-grey scheme for the Phantom. Thus, what if the USMC chose to adopt the black-green-grey camouflage for the Phantom? This model was built with that scenario in mind.

01
DN
158354

01
"Dota"
"Gosmo"
RESCUE
DANGER

01
DN
8354
VMFA-333
MARINES
01

01
DN
8354
158354
VMFA-333
MARINES

VMFA-333
8354
MARINES
01

VMFA-333
8354
MARINES
01
DN
158354

VMFA-333
8354
MARINES
DN
01
158354

Kit: Revell (ex-Hasegawa) Phantom FGR.2
1/48 scale
Kit Ref: Revell 04962
Model by Geoff Coughlin

Aftermarket/Scratch products used:
- Metal foil seat harness
- Photo-etch buckles from an old Reheat photo-etch set
- Wiring to the area between the seats
- Some canopy mirrors

Detailed ejector seats can be a lot of fun to create and you have options here. You can go the easy route which is to buy a couple of resin seats and add those after painting and weathering. The problem is you are likely to have two seats with exactly the same seatbelt arrangement which doesn't look totally authentic.

A couple of nice refinements you can make are to replace the small fillet at the bottom leading edge of the fin and pose the parachute housing (tail cone) open: it's supplied as a separate part and benefits from a bit of detailing. This model has the centreline SUU-23A Vulcan rotary cannon pod added. It looks awesome on the Phantom and was often carried by RAF FGR.2s. Also add the two wing drop tanks.

A paint spatter template was used before adding another thin coat of the Barley grey to blend it in.

The AIM-9L Sidewinders take on many forms when fitted to the British Phantom. So you just need to decide exactly what version you are trying to depict and make them up and finish accordingly. Reference photographs for this aircraft had four AIM-9Ls fitted and all were white with a few stencil markings and the familiar yellow seeker caps. Note the fine retaining cords that secure them in place.

The RAF Phantoms offer the modeller a lot of choice due to their many variations and idiosyncrasies. Looking at the FOD (Foreign Object Damage) guards fitted into the engine intakes on many parked aircraft there are a couple of things to note. The British intakes are different to other marques of Phantom and so had a different design. They are basically simple, flat blanks that have two vertical handles on the front.

With decent references you can add as much or as little as you like. Looking at the kit parts, they are quite good on detail but some important items are missing like the straight rod on each main gear unit that angles back and up from the scissor links. The units did benefit from some small scratched placards too and these were added from metal foil (old wine bottle tops).

Some fine detailing wire is good for representing brake and hydraulic lines. The 'Remove before Flight' tags add a professional finishing touch to the model and the Eduard pre-painted photo-etch ones are excellent. Use the 1/72 scale as the size is a lot more realistic. Equally, if you are building a 1/32 model, use the 1/48 tags. Use thin wire to make a loop in each end and secure the tag to the model.

Check any photos of FGR.2s and you'll see lots of wiring; it looms from behind the seats and these are real features of the type. Adding wiring here will add a level of authenticity the kit parts can't create. You can get lots of different types of fine detailing wire (mostly from model car suppliers). It can easily be bent and shaped; just be careful when handling it as it also breaks easily. Use cyano to secure it all and just work steadily in each area until you have created enough detail.

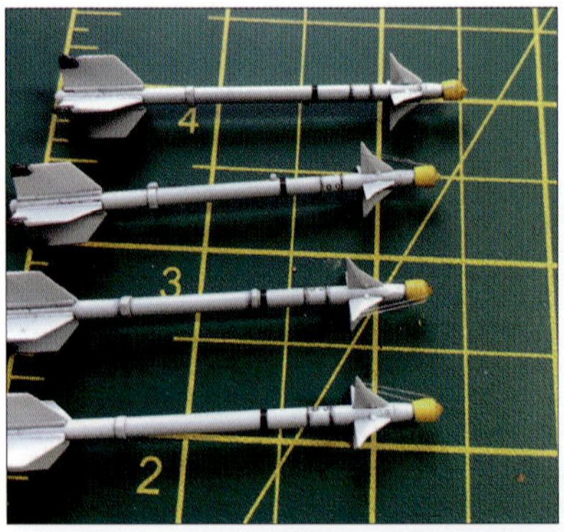

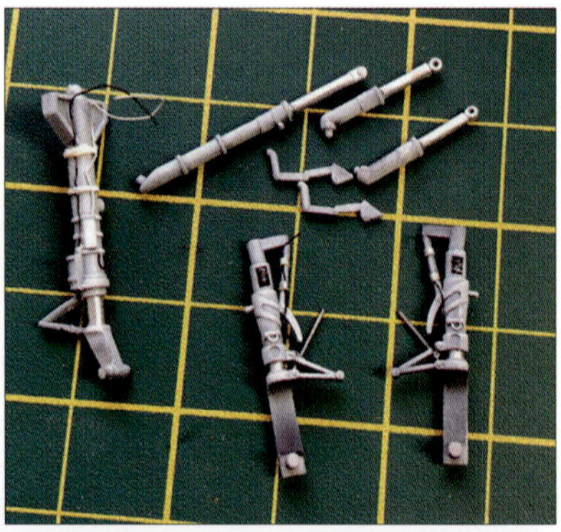

BD
XV470

XV470

XV470
BD

BD
XV470

Further Reading & Bibliography

Chesneau R., *Phantom, McDonnell Phantom FG Mk 1/ FGR Mk 2, Aeroguide 13*, Chipping Ongar, 1986.

Black I., *The Last of The Phantoms*, Yeovil, Patrick Stephens Ltd, 2002.

Black I., *F-4 UK Phantom 1968-1992*, www.firestreakbooks.com, 2020.

Burns M., *McDonnell Douglas F-4K and F-4M Phantom II*, London, Osprey Publishing Ltd, 1984.

Dorr R. F. and Bishop, *Vietnam Air Warfare*, London, Greenwich Editions, 2002.

Dorr R. F. and Bishop, *Vietnam Air War Debrief*, London, Aerospace Publishing Ltd, 1996.

Francillon R. J., *Vietnam Air Wars, French Into China, Laos, Vietnam, Cambodia*, London, Book Club Associates, 1987.

Foster P. R., *RAF Phantom*, Shepperton, Ian Allan Limited, 1989

Hazell S., *McDonnell Douglas F-4K and F-4M Phantom, Warpaint Series No. 31*, Denbigh East, Guideline Publications, 2020.

Hunter J., *Smoke Trails, the Last of the F-4 Phantoms*, Hersham, Midland Publishing, 2007.

Lake J. and Donald, *McDonnell F-4 Phantom, Spirit of the Skies*, USA, AIRtime Publishing Inc, 2002.

Shaw R., *F-4 Phantom, Guardian of the Free World*, Shrewsbury, Airlife Publishing Ltd, 1989.

Stafrace C., *F-4 Phantom II US Navy, US Marine Corps and RAF F-4J(UK)*, Warpaint Series No. 114, Denbigh East, Guideline Publications, 2020.

Thornborough A. M. and Davies, *The Phantom Story*, London, Cassell & Co, 2000.